RECEIVED

JAN 17 2021

ROADVIEW LIBRAR

NO LONGER PROPERTY OF
SEATTLE PUBLIC LIBRARY

D0961281

Break the Good Girl Myth

How to Dismantle
Outdated Rules,
Unleash Your Power,
and Design a More
Purposeful Life

MAJO MOLFINO

Break the Good Girl Myth

HarperOne
An Imprint of HarperCollinsPublishers

HarperOne

I have changed the names of some individuals, including clients, and when needed, modified their identifying features, including physical descriptions, ages and cultural backgrounds, occupations and creative hobbies, as well as geographic locations in order to preserve their anonymity. In some cases, composite characters have been created or timelines have been compressed, in order to further preserve privacy and to maintain narrative flow. The goal in all cases was to protect people's privacy without damaging the integrity of the anecdotes and their lessons.

BREAK THE GOOD GIRL MYTH. Copyright © 2020 by Majo Molfino. All rights reserved. Printed in the United States of America. No part of this book may be used or reproduced in any manner whatsoever without written permission except in the case of brief quotations embodied in critical articles and reviews. For information, address HarperCollins Publishers, 195 Broadway, New York, NY 10007.

HarperCollins books may be purchased for educational, business, or sales promotional use. For information, please email the Special Markets Department at SPsales@harpercollins.com.

FIRST EDITION

Designed by Janet Evans-Scanlon

Illustrations by Vanessa Koch

Library of Congress Cataloging-in-Publication Data
Names: Molfino, Majo, author.
Title: Break the good girl myth : how to dismantle outdated rules, unleash your power, and design a more purposeful life / Majo Molfino.
Description: First edition. | New York, NY : HarperOne, [2020]
Identifiers: LCCN 2019047928 (print) | LCCN 2019047929 (ebook) | ISBN 9780062894052 | ISBN 9780062894076 (ebook)
Subjects: LCSH: Self-esteem in women. | Feminism. | Patriarchy.
Classification: LCC BF697.5.S46 M53 2020 (print) | LCC BF697.5.S46 (ebook) | DDC 155.3/3391—dc23
LC record available at https://lccn.loc.gov/2019047928
LC ebook record available at https://lccn.loc.gov/2019047929

---

20 21 22 23 24 LSC 10 9 8 7 6 5 4 3 2 1

For my mother and her mother and her mother . . .

Don't ask me what I did. Ask me what I did not do.
I did not clip her wings, and that's all.

—ZIAUDDIN YOUSAFZAI,
Malala Yousafzai's father

Contents

Author's Note

I'VE MOSTLY DRAWN ON MY OWN LIFE AND THOSE OF MY CLIENTS and friends, as well as my podcast guests and listeners, to show how the good girl archetype exists. The details of my clients' lives have been rearranged, changed, or merged into composite personas in an effort to anonymize them. Though the women included in this book represent a small slice of the world, I believe the good girl is universal and speaks to women from a wide range of experiences and walks of life. My hope is that you see parts of yourself reflected here, regardless of how you identify or where you come from as a woman.

1
Becoming the Good Girl

SITTING ON MY DESK IS A PHOTOGRAPH OF MYSELF AT AGE twelve. It was my first day at an all-girls Catholic high school in Montreal, Canada. I stood at the bottom of a stairwell, gripping the straps of my backpack. I wore a plaid blue-green skirt, and my black shoes were so impeccably polished that you could see the camera flash in them. My hair was tied back in the tightest of ponytails. Doing this was my effort to fit in more and to make the other girls like me. I was a very good girl.

I was a daughter of immigrants and a straight A+ student, but underneath this perfect, good girl persona was a darker truth: I didn't know where I belonged. Though I was born in Buenos Aires, I couldn't tell you on what street or in which neighborhood we lived, or about the smell of leather and cigarettes that flooded the kiosks, because my parents decided to immigrate to Canada when I was only a baby. I can't speak Spanish more than conversationally, and I have trouble remembering some very basic words. While my aunts, uncles, and grandmothers still live in Argentina, I didn't grow up with them and generally felt disconnected from my roots, language, culture, and community.

In my childhood years, I caved in to peer pressures and wanted desperately to be like my blonde, blue-eyed Canadian friends with perfectly English–sounding names like Allison and Rebecca. I was embarrassed that my parents spoke English with a heavy accent (worrying that people thought we were stupid) and that we didn't know what sleepovers and Halloween were, customs we didn't have in Argentina. I hated being teased about my full name, Maria José. Kids would often taunt "No way, José! No way, José!" or my friends' parents would break out into the song "Maria" from *West Side Story*, a reference I little knew or cared about.

I was different, and I felt it. Though I had loving parents, by the time I was fifteen, I had attended ten different schools and lived in at least six different houses and towns in Canada and the United States. Put plainly, being a good, determined, high-achieving daughter of immigrants was my safest way to assimilate and cope with the ineffable loss, grief, and lack of belonging and connection I felt in my heart.

That's a Good Girl

There's something instantly recognizable about the good girl, isn't there? She's the girl in a schoolgirl uniform. She's the girl who plays classical piano or practices ballet for years at the insistence of her parents. She's the girl who wins the spelling bee. She's the girl who does her homework. She's the girl who is sweet, naïve, and docile. There's a reason these images come to mind when we think of her. It's because she's truly familiar and universal. It's because our society has conditioned too many of us to believe that we will be rewarded only when we are being nice, playing by the rules, and working hard.

While it's true that the good girl is a universal phenomenon, it's also true that you have your own unique good girl journey. Whether you've considered yourself a typical good girl in the past or not, I assure you that we all have glimpses of her within us. For me, the good girl manifested herself primarily through my performance at school and, later in life, through my performance at work. But I also wanted boys to love me, giving me the attention and approval I desperately craved. As a teenager, when I got attention from popular boys in school—you know, the bad boys, troublemakers, and class clowns—it led me into some seriously bad relationships, even into my twenties (more on that later).

For you, the good girl will find her own unique expression. But for all of us, her roots can be traced back to a common source: the patriarchy. Like armor or a mask, the good girl archetype is a protective mechanism, a way to be that helps us feel safe and loved in the patriarchy but that is ultimately disempowering.

What's the patriarchy? That old thing is a (very annoying) social and cultural system that privileges men, in visible and invisible ways, over women and other genders.* It's pretty much everywhere, like the air we breathe and the water we drink. Under its foot, we become good girls who compromise our needs and desires in order to survive, fit in, and be accepted, paying the price by giving up our fulfillment and power. Indeed, the good girl is that domesticated part of ourselves that has been tamed and trained by this system over our entire lifetime and perhaps even over multiple generations of women in our families. When we embody her, we play it safe, hold back our voices, and don't share our true gifts with the world.

---

* This book is written for anyone who identifies as a woman, whether they were assigned that gender at birth or not. When I use the term *men*, I'm referring to cisgender, heteronormative men. Although this book is written for those who self-identify as women, the patriarchy also harms several marginalized groups, such as homosexual and transgendered men, in various ways. And while the patriarchy privileges cis, hetero men over other genders, it simultaneously harms them too, which I'll talk about in the next section.

The Patriarchy

I've found that the word *feminism*, like *patriarchy*, has gained a bad reputation—not surprisingly, in the patriarchy! As one podcast listener told me, "I'm allergic to that word. I think of an angry feminist who burns bras and points her finger at men, when the issue is a lot more complicated. It just feels accusatory." Steering clear of words like *feminism* and *patriarchy* makes our good girl feel safe, since we aren't ruffling any bow ties. Let's make sure we're all on the same page about what I mean when I say *patriarchy*, which will give context for understanding the good girl.

The patriarchy is a system of oppression. Oppression is unjust treatment and control by another—whether it's an individual, a group, or an entire social and cultural system. A key assumption of this book is that we're born into cultures that oppress us based on specific factors, such as gender, race, and economic status. There are more, but we'll keep this simple for our purposes. In many parts of the world, girls and women continue to be oppressed and denied their rights to education or health care or are forced into labor or the sex trade. In the United States, Latina, Native American, and Black women are paid far less than are white non-Hispanic men *for the exact same work.*[1]

Some forms of oppression are obvious and loud, some are subtle and quiet, but either way, they exist. The opposite of oppression is freedom, power, and choice. The opposite of being oppressed is having privilege. When I first heard someone call me privileged, I became defensive, but I soon came to see they were right: being white, wealthier than most, and able-bodied gave me more privilege than those without these qualities and affordances. I discovered I was not only in the "oppressed" category as a woman but also in the "oppressor" category as a woman with privilege. This can feel like an uncomfortable pill to swallow, but doing this type of internal work is often uncomfortable, so gear up. Each and every one of us oppresses and is oppressed. It's good to own both sides because then we can see the ways we are deeply hurt (by the patriarchy, obviously) *and* the ways we unconsciously hurt others by having more privilege and power.

The patriarchy is inside you. Are you surprised by this? Many women think the patriarchy is something imposed on them externally, but whenever we live inside a system that oppresses us, that system lives inside us too. We begin to internalize its messages (more on messengers later) and often mistake those messages for our own thoughts. Our inner patriarchs direct a portion of our subconscious thoughts, words, and behaviors, which stop us from becoming our authentic selves. The main premise of this book is that the patriarchy is inside you and manifests as the good girl, but you can do something about it and reclaim your power.

The patriarchy has friends. Classically, when we say *patriarchy*, we're talking about oppression based on gender. But the truth is that the patriarchy plays and intersects with other systems that exclude groups of people, namely, white supremacy, which oppresses people of color, based on race, and typically says light skin is better than dark skin; and capitalism, which oppresses low-income people, based on economic status, and says high-income is better than low-income.* Think about these systems of oppression as bolstering and enhancing each other, playing each other up like good old

---

* Free markets aren't inherently bad. In America today, however, capitalism lives on unchecked as corporations gain more power and influence over people and communities and we prioritize commodifying and extracting the Earth's resources over regenerating them.

pals in a smoking parlor. I don't have enough space here to get into the intricacies of the patriarchy and all its vast intersections every time I mention it—so just assume when I say *patriarchy*, I'm taking on an inclusive and intersectional view of it as today's current, dominant mainstream culture, which includes a dangerous brew of other systems of oppression as well.

The patriarchy is old. The patriarchy has existed for as long as we've had language—since about 3100 BC. If there was anything besides the patriarchy in our prehistoric lives, we certainly don't have any written records of it. However, the anthropologist Marija Gimbutas studied the folk art and artifacts of Old Europe and concluded there was a long epoch (about 7000–3500 BC) *before* written history when people lived in a more egalitarian agricultural society.[2] She concluded they worshipped the Earth and depicted her cycles and fertility through Goddess art and figurines, but a brutal invasion by Indo-European warriors north of the Baltic Sea wiped them out and set the basis for the patriarchal Western culture and language we have today.[3] In recent years, DNA evidence has emerged to suggest she was spot-on about this invasion.[4] Whether her theory is true or not, one thing's for sure: the patriarchy has been around us for thousands of years, since the beginnings of written civilization, and still exists among us today, decades after the women's liberation movement of the 1960s.

The patriarchy is everywhere. It is our current state of affairs and exists everywhere on the planet. All contemporary culture is built on a system that oppresses girls, women, and basically anyone who doesn't identify as a male. So, if you're a woman born anytime in the past five thousand years, the patriarchy is all around you. And perhaps I don't need to sound the alarm bell too loudly, because it feels a little more obvious in recent times thanks to the public outing of sexual harassment in Hollywood, in Silicon Valley, and (cough) by Donald Trump. Maybe it feels obvious thanks to the bleak reality that women still make up only 4.8 percent of the CEOs at Fortune 500 companies;[5] 20 percent of all directors, writers, producers, and editors of top films;[6] and 23.7 percent of congressional representatives.[7] But just to make sure we're all on the same page: by and large men, not women, are still at the helm of all major decisions, policy, technology, and culture making in the world. You can find the patriarchy in your kitchen cupboard; on your shampoo bottles, baby clothes, shoes, favorite movies, songs, and tech products; and at any stores near you. With the click of a button, swipe of a credit card, or even sniff of the nose, there it is—the patriarchy is ready to seep into your mind-body and work its dangerous magic on you.

Yes, some cultures are more patriarchal than others. There are some female-positive, matrifocal societies and cultures, but they tend to be isolated, sparse, and tribal instead of widespread, and many of them still have taboos about menstruation, which has led quite a few anthropologists to claim there is no proof of a true matriarchal society (highly debated!). The point is that there has never been a widespread matriarchy as pervasively as there has been a widespread patriarchy. And, to be honest, I'm not even voting for a matriarchy. What I want is something more fundamental: an egalitarian world in which we are more connected to ourselves, each other, and the planet. I have a feeling you do too.

The patriarchy hurts all of us. The focus of this book is women, but the patriarchy also hurts men. While women are told to be good girls, men are pressured to be aggressive, macho, athletic, insensitive, womanizing . . . you get the drift. Worst of all, the patriarchy negatively affects children because we force them into a gender binary, give them toys based on their gender, and train them to fulfill harsh, one-size-fits-all gender norms instead of giving them a chance to express who they truly are. Since the patriarchy says the white man is at the very top of the food chain and that man is smarter than nature (ha!), it also justifies groups in power destroying and dominating people who are, or who are seen as, more connected to nature. History shows this devastation demonstrated by the European conquest and colonization of indigenous peoples around the globe. Of course, this dominance extends over animals, plant life, and the Earth's natural resources. The patriarchy gives humans the perfect justification to dominate, eradicate, and extract from Mother Earth.

The patriarchy has messengers. The patriarchy is not a single individual or group of people (i.e., "all men"). It's synonymous with dominant culture, which means it trickles down invisibly into our communities and subcultures. When something is so invisible, it needs physical messengers. These messengers are the communities we grow up in and their members. When we're growing up, we're extremely susceptible to messengers, which come in so many shape-shifting forms, making them hard to catch. They are those we worship who are close to us (e.g., parents) and those we worship from far away (e.g., celebrities).

Keep in mind, messengers are not evil. Goddess, no! Most of the time, they don't even know they're being messengers on behalf of the patriarchy. Please read carefully: messengers aren't necessarily men. Messengers can be of any gender, age, sexual orientation, religious affiliation, race, or ethnicity. Without getting too philosophical on you, we're all messengers of culture for each other. We *all* spread culture around like melted butter on toast. We all carry around toxic ideas about women and femininity that we need to unlearn. What I like about this metaphor of a messenger is that it allows us to have more compassion for everybody involved. No one is inherently bad. We're all duped by the patriarchy. The problem isn't a person but a destructive system we need to dismantle together. To sum up, the patriarchy isn't a single bad guy you can point to, but it finds human vessels through which to keep sharing its message. Throughout the book, when you find me talking about how the patriarchy developed each of the Good Girl Myths, I'll back it up by pointing to one or more of the following messengers, listed in the table on the next page.

Of course, there could be more messengers, depending on where and how you grew up, but in my experience these are the four main groups to look out for. The point is that we all have unique players that shape us into the patriarchy's dolls. We'll dive more into how these messengers work their sneaky magic on us in the first Good Girl Myth, but I want to convey this core concept that the patriarchy oozes its way into other people, who in turn send us negative messages, whether knowingly or unknowingly, and shape us into good girls.

Designing Our Way Out of This

I want to help you break the spell of the Good Girl Myths because I'm a good girl in *serious* recovery. I was that little girl who eagerly touched her "head, shoulders, knees and toes, knees and toes," with hearts in my eyes for my teachers. I was that girl who sat in the front of the classroom and, when the teacher asked a question,

Tribe or Culture	Description	Its Messengers
Family	The familial tribe you were born into and grew up in—those you spent most time with during your early years	Parents and primary caregivers obviously have the biggest impact on a child's life. Moms have particularly huge effects on their daughters. But other members can also uphold and spread the patriarchy's message, such as grandparents, fathers, siblings, cousins, aunts, uncles, and other extended family members.
School	All the schools—from elementary to college—that you attended	The main authority figures here are teachers, counselors, coaches, and other students' parents. Our friends and peers also profoundly shape us.
Religion	The religion and spiritual tradition you were born into and grew up in, especially during your early years	Leaders in the community who have more access to texts and knowledge tend to have more power. Think priests, nuns, rabbis, preachers, and other community members and organizers.
Pop culture	Larger Western mainstream pop culture and entertainment such as television, news, film, magazines, and music you consumed, especially in your early years	Messengers here are any celebrities such as actors, musicians, models, British royalty, fashion designers, artists, and other culture makers. You know, the rich, beautiful, and famous. In the age of the internet, these messengers have access to little girls more than ever before.

shot her arm up so hard and fast that it almost dislocated. *Please pick me, PLEASE!* I've been called a brownnoser, whistleblower (hey, every classroom needs them), and teacher's pet. Anything for a gold star. As a Latina and an immigrant, I was terrified of disappointing my parents, who had left their home country and sacrificed so much for me.

By the time I had been through school, I had become a total rule-follower and felt completely disconnected from my creativity. So it's no surprise that after college, I landed in a boring 9-to-5 cubicle job as a research assistant and felt deflated, disengaged, and depressed—a rock-bottom time in my life that led to a bunch of soul searching—and eventually I decided to enroll in a master's program in learning, design, and technology at Stanford University. This program was a real turning point for me because I learned design thinking (more on design thinking in just a moment) and developed what design thinkers call *creative confidence*, which had a huge positive impact on my career and overall well-being. I began doing what I loved to do as a little girl (you know, long before the pressure of getting grades started), such as writing poetry, fiction, and music, all of which led me to eventually start a coaching business, launch a podcast, and land a book deal with a renowned publisher. If I was still being a good girl, afraid of sharing my gifts and voice, I wouldn't have been able to do all these amazing things. Through my own experience, I realized that design, especially in combination with other modalities, could be a powerful tool to support women in counteracting their good-girl conditioning and living their fullest lives.

Today, I support other women in overcoming their Good Girl Myths so that they can start businesses; question their superiors; transfer to more aligned companies and teams; get raises; write

13

books, songs, and manifestos; or, fuck it, finally take that hard-earned guilt-free sabbatical so they can start painting again. Because if there's anything the Good Girl Myths do, it's stop a woman from tapping into her creative life force and embracing change, discomfort, and the unknown—ingredients that lead to a badass life.

So what is design and design thinking? Many times we think of design strictly in terms of the world's highly creative industries, such as fashion, interior, and graphic design, but it extends far beyond that. *Everything* can be designed. Design isn't only about aesthetics and beauty; it's about making systems and experiences work better for us.

Design thinking is a process that involves deeply understanding people's needs, synthesizing our observations, and brainstorming, prototyping, and testing solutions multiple times before coming up with the best design. What I love about it is that it's both powerful and flexible. For example, after hours of observing women paint their nails, designers at the design firm IDEO noticed a persistent problem: one hand is way easier to paint than the other—ladies, you know exactly what I'm talking about. This insight led them to design a nail polish bottle with a bendy wand so that the less dominant hand can have better control and precision.[8] Genius, I know. Using exactly the same design thinking process, a group of students from Stanford's Hasso Plattner Institute of Design, known as the d.school, designed a low-cost incubator for babies around the world. Instructors challenged them to come up with a baby warmer that would cost less than 1 percent of the cost of traditional incubators so it would be affordable in impoverished communities.[9] So, as you can see, from designing better nail polish bottles to saving the lives of three hundred thousand premature babies, design is fundamentally a way of approaching human problems and needs. In the same way, it can be applied to the bigger questions of our lives, such as our lifestyles, careers, and relationships. In fact, I'd say *you* are your biggest design project. As authors and design thinkers Bill Burnet and Dave Evans wrote in *Designing Your Life: How to Build a Well-Lived, Joyful Life*, "you can use the same thinking that created the most amazing technology, products, and spaces to design your career and your life."[10]

Indeed, design thinking helped me come up with the Good Girl Myths framework and understand how to overcome these myths. In this book, I'll show you exactly how each myth impacts your work, relationships, and well-being and provide you with tools based on design thinking to make a real difference in your life, right away. We're going to think and approach problems as designers do.

Let's start with some key mind-sets inspired by design thinking that I've specifically tailored for good girls. These mind-sets are as follows:

1. Seek deeper understanding.

Empathy is the foundation of all good design. It's the act of putting ourselves in another person's shoes. Designers listen, observe, and understand other people's true needs; otherwise, they would be designing based on their assumptions (what they think others need) rather than reality (what others truly need). Without empathy, design becomes shallow and offers Band-Aid solutions. As we peel back our good girl layers, we're going to need to seek a deeper understanding of ourselves by being curious about our wants and needs and what truly matters to us in this lifetime. We start with having empathy for ourselves and how we got here, not placing blame or shame, and believing we have unlimited potential for growth.

2. Open your mind.

Clients come to me because they feel stuck or lost in their careers and relationships. They're often not *actually* stuck, but they need to see and generate more options for themselves and to believe those options are possible. In design thinking, being generative—that is, ideating and brainstorming—allows us to think and draw outside the lines, which many of us good girls have long forgotten how to do! Opening your mind also involves reframing any core dysfunctional beliefs about yourself and the world.

3. Make something.

Once we've generated options for ourselves, we have to put them into practice, and we do this through prototyping. If you're feeling stuck and happen to be roaming the halls of the d.school, it wouldn't be surprising to hear an instructor or director tell you to pick up some cardboard, foam, or tape and make something (honestly, *anything*) with your hands. Making something sparks new ideas and enables us to learn much faster. I'll get more into prototyping in our first chapters, but just know that the way we gain clarity is by making small, dinky versions of our ideas and putting them out into the world, not by overthinking them in our heads. Design thinking teaches us that we gain clarity and confidence through *action*. Perfect for you perfectionists!

4. Engage someone.

We can make something and stuff it into our closet, never, ever telling anyone about it, *or* we can put it in front of someone and see how they respond. Asking for feedback, as well as giving it, is a key component of design thinking, which is highly collaborative. *Asking for feedback*, whether from a friend, acquaintance, total stranger, or possible future customer, may make us feel vulnerable but is key in both discovering and carving a path that's meaningful to us. In the same vein, continuously *giving* feedback and using our voices, instead of staying quiet on a subject, is essential to having healthy relationships, in both our personal lives and our work lives.

5. Set yourself up for success.

I've applied design thinking to behavior change for many years now and have learned we often can't rely on willpower to create change. Instead, we need to set ourselves up for success, and more specifically, we need to design our environments to make new behaviors easier. This involves setting up our physical space to align with the life we want to create but also putting accountability into place to ensure we take the steps we want to take but may be too afraid to.

Using these mind-sets inspired by design thinking, we'll set ourselves and our surroundings up to dismantle these myths and create a whole new system that gives us agency and power.

On my podcast, HEROINE, I've interviewed a wide range of illustrious women, such as author and activist Isabel Allende, fashion icon and entrepreneur Eileen Fisher, culture critic and digital strategist Luvvie Ajayi, psychotherapist and thought leader Esther Perel, design educator Debbie Millman, letterer and type designer Jessica Hische, and award-winning photojournalist Lynsey Addario. These women have helped me understand what makes a heroine, which is basically my word for a creative female badass who has largely broken away from her Good Girl Myths. It describes women who take risks, embrace the unknown, and share their voices. For an even fuller understanding of what it can look like when we dismantle these myths and live out our power, I urge you to complement your reading here with episodes from the podcast by visiting HEROINE.fm.

Finally, as a seeker of truth, I've studied and trained in various yogic traditions in the past decade, taught stress-management courses at the Stanford School of Medicine, and practice meditation and mindfulness regularly. I weave a more holistic perspective into my coaching and guidance and blend these modalities with the more action-oriented approach of design thinking. I want you to be and feel empowered on *all* levels—mind, body, heart, and soul. That's what we need if we're going to break free. But please know that regardless of your belief system, you're totally welcome here.

All I ask is that you come into this journey with an open mind, ready to roll up your sleeves and get to work. If you take this adventure with me, you're going to discover what's blocking you from sharing your gifts with the world and what's holding back your power as a woman on this planet today. The Good Girl Myths, in all their sneakiness, may have followed you into adulthood, but you can do something about it *today.*

This book is your guide to breaking free from the good girl.

2

The
Good Girl
Myths

IF YOU'RE BEGINNING TO REALIZE HOW DEEP YOUR GOOD girl conditioning runs, and all the ways the patriarchy has been stealing your power, don't worry. You're not alone. I've seen the good girl displayed in each of my clients, who are all smart, ambitious women, some of whom work at the world's most innovative companies. I've seen her in the stories of top female leaders and creative risk-takers whom I've interviewed on my podcast. I've seen her in the messages I receive from readers and listeners who say, "Oh, I'm such a goodie," and "I'm trying to recover from this good girl thing. Help!" And, of course, I'm a recovering good girl as well! Regardless of her age or level of success, or whether she's from Brazil, the United Kingdom, or Japan, I've met the good girl time and time again. She may feel familiar to you too. It's likely that you've been developing your good girl for years, maybe even decades, having spent countless Thanksgivings listening to Uncle Harold tell you to wait your turn to speak.

Even though the good girl looks different for each of us, she takes on the same five shapes, which I call the five Good Girl Myths and which are the core self-sabotaging beliefs that hold you back and suffocate your power as a strong, confident woman. They're part of a dusty, outdated set of expectations that pressure women to be obedient, small, and self-sacrificing instead of powerful and revolutionary. The good news is that you're far from alone, and there's a way to reverse the spell of your myths. We'll just need some raven's claw, rosemary, and a mini cauldron. Just kidding! I truly believe that if you make your way through the pages of this book, we'll learn together how to recognize and unlearn the Good Girl Myths. Because, trust me, they're sneaky motherfuckers.

You can think of each Good Girl Myth as a software program, installed by the patriarchy, that runs in the background without your realizing it. The patriarchy and its messengers install disempowering programs of thoughts, beliefs, and behaviors when we're impressionable little girls. These programs are largely subconscious and follow us into adulthood. The Good Girl Myths aren't wholly disempowering, however. Each myth has the potential to come into balance and work in our favor, which I'll get into later, but for now we'll focus on how they're blocking us. Let's take a look at each of the Good Girl Myths in turn.

The Myth of Rules

SOUNDS LIKE
"If I follow the rules, life will be easier and I will get ahead."

LOOKS LIKE
The tendency to seek and follow external rules and authority instead of trusting our own desires, needs, and opinions.

MAIN STRATEGY FOR APPROVAL
Being good and following others' expectations.

POWERS YOU GIVE UP
Your purpose and self-authority.

The Myth of Perfection

SOUNDS LIKE

"I must perform at a high level in all areas of my life without breaking a sweat."

LOOKS LIKE

The tendency to demand perfection in ourselves and others instead of embracing mistakes and the reality of how things are.

MAIN STRATEGY FOR APPROVAL

Being the best at everything and better than others.

POWERS YOU GIVE UP

Your creative confidence, vulnerability, and authenticity.

The Myth of Logic

SOUNDS LIKE

"It's best to follow my mind and intellect over my body and intuition."

LOOKS LIKE

The tendency to choose logic over intuition in decision making.

MAIN STRATEGY FOR APPROVAL

Being smart and credible.

POWERS YOU GIVE UP

Your intuition, imagination, and empathy.

The Myth of Harmony

SOUNDS LIKE

"If I just go with the flow and avoid being difficult, there won't be any problems and everyone will just get along."

LOOKS LIKE

The tendency to seek and keep harmony instead of embracing the conflict and confrontation needed for change.

MAIN STRATEGY FOR APPROVAL

Being easy to get along with, pleasant, and likable.

POWERS YOU GIVE UP

Your voice and truth.

The Myth of Sacrifice

SOUNDS LIKE

"I should prioritize the needs of others before my own."

LOOKS LIKE

The tendency to put other people's needs above your own at the expense of your self-care and well-being.

MAIN STRATEGY FOR APPROVAL

Being selfless, helpful, and saving the day.

POWERS YOU GIVE UP

Your time and energy, which add up to your contribution and destiny.

There you have it. The Good Girl Myths: Rules, Perfection, Logic, Harmony, and Sacrifice. As you can see, each myth sounds and looks unique, and each is a totally self-defeating strategy for approval and survival in the patriarchy. These strategies are self-defeating because the more you attempt to make them work, the further away you are from connection, belongingness, and fulfillment, which is what you actually desire. When we're under the spell of the Good Girl Myths, we deny other parts of ourselves that need and want expression. We deny ourselves our full power and potential, which is why they're so dangerous.

Taking Apart the Myths in Our Lives

By identifying the Good Girl Myths, you'll start to realize the invisible powers that have been at work over the course of your life, and you'll start to take them apart one by one, rebuilding a new, healthy, powerful way of being in and contributing to the world. Here are the ways doing this work can help you.

Quiet the Patriarchy Inside You

Listen, there's no doubt that we must work to change the patriarchy around us through activism, civic engagement, and political action. We can't simply "self-help away" injustices. But the focus of *this* book is dismantling the patriarchy *inside* ourselves. Though we certainly aren't to blame for being oppressed, we are responsible for freeing ourselves. Responsibility, not blame. There's a key difference! This book is asking you to take full responsibility for your freedom, without guilt or shame. To take your life into your own hands. You know the way Gandhi talked about it? "Be the change," he said. And that man was no fool. He helped free India from British rule without any violence whatsoever. He believed *the personal was the political*. As such, if you take the time to do this inner work, you'll become more powerful and even more effective in any actions you take in the world. As the cliché goes, you'll walk the walk, not just talk the talk. This book will show you what you can do as a woman, right now, to become more powerful. *That is a political act.* You *can* work on understanding how the patriarchy lives inside you and begin managing it. You have a ton of agency over that. And that's a big deal.

Shed Light on Your Subconscious

Right now, your conscious mind might say, "Majo, I want to be a badass—let's do this!" But as you go about your life, doing your best to be a badass, you run into walls. Your job at the hospital sucks up all your time, and living in Chicago is super expensive, and dating feels impossible, and, and, and . . . It seems like the world is out to get you, and there are too many barriers (outside you, of course) that are stopping you from achieving full badassery. Right? Wrong. You've got some swampy creatures, a.k.a. self-sabotaging beliefs, living right below the line of your awareness.

The Good Girl Myths are self-sabotaging beliefs that lurk in the murky waters of your subconscious mind. Because you were born into the patriarchy, these disempowering beliefs have lodged in your subconscious since you were a babe and have pitched their tents all over your turf. This book will show you exactly how each myth sounds and impacts different areas of your life, particularly your work, relationships, and well-being.

Though I've done my best to make this an easy read, it's far from a comfortable one, since I'll be asking you to look at parts of yourself that don't look great under the limelight (it's okay; we all have them). I promise you that any short-term discomfort is worth the long-term payoff—more growth and self-knowledge. This book will help you bring your subconscious tendencies out of the shadows and into the light, so that we can make real change.

Discover Your Primary Good Girl Myth

All of us are under the spell of the Good Girl Myths, but because of our unique personalities and histories, each myth grips some of us more than others. There may be one particular myth that you find yourself coming back to again and again, or that you instantly know, *Yes, that one has me in its palm.* You can consider that one your primary Good Girl Myth. Check out chapter 3 for a self-assessment that will help you determine what your primary Good Girl Myth is. But understand that while most of us do tend to have one or two myths that we struggle with more than the others, all of them will contribute to that "inner patriarchy" I mentioned earlier. So it's crucial that you read through all five myths to clearly see where you might need to do some work.

Your primary myth is also the one that you will find the hardest to overcome. Because of my desire to belong and achieve, my primary Good Girl Myth is the Myth of Perfection. My biggest shadows have to do with competition, comparison, and wanting to be number one. At my worst, I can be so concerned about self-image and achievement that I will forgo my more authentic passions of poetry, fiction, and music. The Myth of Logic is a close second for me. Since my academic training was so rigorous, it beefed up my intellect far more than my body's intelligence. I find it hard to stay embodied and grounded throughout the day. But every woman is different. One client, Sandra, a designer at an agency who had trouble expressing what she wanted and needed from her co-workers and boss, was under the Myth of Harmony. Agatha, a former Catholic, finds she willingly gives up her authority and can't trust herself when making decisions. Her primary myth is the Myth of Rules. Beatrice, an executive assistant to a CEO who always puts her own needs last, is mostly under the spell of the Myth of Sacrifice. In other words, even though you possess all the myths, discovering your primary Good Girl Myth will give you a direction in which to focus your energy.

Come Back to Center

This may sound counterintuitive, but it's an important caveat: there isn't anything inherently wrong with any of the Good Girl Myths. I do *not* believe we should eliminate rules, logic, harmony, sacrifice, or even perfection in this world, nor is it necessarily a problem to be upholding these qualities from time to time. But because we're trying to better understand your conditioning, I *will* spend quite a bit of time talking about how and why the myths are so dangerous. After we travel through the negative layers together, I'll reveal the inherent potential within each myth when it's well integrated. After all, qualities such as harmony and logic have their place. The problem is that as good girls, we've swung too much in one direction, and we need to swing the pendulum back toward the center so that we can become powerful. But let's definitely not throw the baby out with the bathwater! Let's just add a little more balance into the mix.

Experience More Choice

Again, the myths, and even being a good girl, aren't inherently bad. I get frustrated when I find myself or others looking down on housewives. Is that why we had the feminist movement? So we can look down on other women? No. Feminism is about choice. It's not that you have to be a housewife; it's that you *get to be* one *if you want to*. In the same way, it's not that you shouldn't follow rules anymore; it's that you get to follow rules *if you want to*. It's not that you shouldn't be harmonious; it's that you get to be harmonious *if you want to*. When we're humming along without any awareness about our subconscious self-sabotaging tendencies, we don't see very many options to choose differently. When we become aware of the myths, we get to choose differently, and sometimes we will still choose to be a good girl. And that's okay. At least we made the choice and didn't fall into a pattern we were unaware of. This distinction is subtle but makes all the difference.

Take Action

I became a coach and designer because I believe in the power of learning through action. As much as I love all the inspiration stuff, this book is about giving you some practical tools you can put to good use. As I noted on pages 15–17, many of the mind-sets we'll discuss are inspired by design thinking and include getting out of your head and into the world by making something (e.g., prototyping) and engaging someone (e.g., getting feedback). Expect each Good Girl Myth to have a unique set of mind-sets and tools because each one has a different way of pooping on your party. And expect me to challenge you to self-reflect and interact with the world. Throughout the book, keep your eye open for exercises marked by this special icon ⬡ challenging you to dig deep, externalize your thoughts, and go make something happen in the real world. I also recommend that you work through the exercises in a journal that you specifically dedicate to this book. You're getting access to stuff my private clients pay thousands of dollars for, so pay attention and do the work if you want results!

Discover More You

We've discussed many of the negatives around how girls have been conditioned by the patriarchy, but little girls also have the benefit of being unapologetic, fully owning who they are. Have you ever noticed that some old ladies are this way too? That's where we're going. Some call it soul; some call it the essential, original, or native self. I don't care what you call it. It's the place inside you that neither culture nor trauma has damaged. When you came into this planet, you were a mini-Goddess—capable of basically anything. You were naturally creative, powerful, and free. One hundred percent yourself.

When I interview a woman about her story, the first question I ask is "What were you like as a little girl?" It's a deceptively simple question, but it gives us clues about what we were like *before* we became good girls. As one client shared in reflecting on her girlhood, "I was always dancing, doing cartwheels, playing with beads, writing, drawing, making stuff with friends, bossing people around, or having my nose in a book. The more I can close that circle, the happier I am."

Another client shared the before and after of when her good girl conditioning creeped in: "When I was really little (four to six), I'd dress up and rearrange my room so I could host my own talk show (channeling my inner Oprah). When I got a little older, I became a perfectionist. If I colored outside the lines, I'd abandon the page and start again on the next." There was *once* an authentic self who played make-believe, unafraid of what others thought of her. With patriarchal conditioning, that voice became quiet and distant. She is like an inward-curling jasmine flower in a dark corner we need to shed some moonlight on. We want her to *return* to her wise and bold self.

There's no doubt that you're on a journey—and not just any kind of journey but one known as the *heroine's journey.* Unlike the hero who goes out and battles the outer demons of the world, the heroine looks inward and befriends her inner demons to come out on the other side more integrated and powerful. The heroine's journey is about reclaiming ourselves and, particularly, our feminine power. The next chapter will help you look inward to discover what myths are gripping you the most and what areas you most need to reclaim.

Know this: By journeying through the Good Girl Myths and becoming more you, you will naturally cause a ripple, a riot, a revolution within. You will come alive. You will create the radically new. You will bring about what the world needs instead of the good girl the world thinks it wants. And if that feels overwhelming, remember that you're not alone. You're weaving one vital thread in a larger tapestry of millions. We need all hands on deck.

3

What Kind of Good Girl Are You?

DISCOVERING YOUR PRIMARY GOOD GIRL MYTH IS ES-
sential to stepping into your power. Even though we
are susceptible to all the myths to some degree, there
is one myth that runs the deepest in your subconscious and is the
loudest in your life.

It's worth noting that the primary Good Girl Myths are not
fixed personality traits but programs of conditioning. For some
of us, our primary myth is fluid and changes depending on our
context, such as our developmental stage, life area, or relationship
dynamic. Sometimes we break through a primary myth in a given
life phase, leaving room for another to take the lead. A friend
shared beautifully about this experience: "In elementary school
and high school, I was all about science, and logic was the holy
grail. I broke through that once I started doing dance again, but
when I graduated, I was terrified to claim myself as a contemporary dancer, so I went into a nine-to-five to please my folks, which
is basically Rules. Once I got through *that*, I had kids, and now
Sacrifice keeps popping up, since that's how my mom was with
my siblings and me."

Our primary myth can also be fluid in terms of life area. We
may be run by Perfection at work but dominated by Harmony in
our relationships. Alternatively, we may find it hard to speak up
in a work context (Harmony) yet find that we make our romantic
decisions in a way that fulfills family and cultural expectations
(Rules). Your primary myth may even change depending on who
you're in relationship with. If you're a highly adaptable woman,
you might notice that for whatever reason, in a specific relationship

or friendship, you are completely gripped by Sacrifice (the feeling that you should put yourself last), but in another relationship, you are the "practical" one and following Logic, perhaps in reaction to your fear that the other person won't or can't. Such is the changing, fluid reality of nature—we do our best to capture it with labels, but can we ever, really?

So yes, for some of us, our primary myth changes. For others, however, a myth can feel relentless and overwhelmingly omnipresent. Take Hannah, who we'll hear more from in the Myth of Harmony chapter. Because of how and where she grew up and her early encounters with her father, she can't remember a time when standing up for herself felt easy. This primary myth has been her lifelong challenge, and though it's gotten more manageable through our coaching, it's still the myth she has to keep her eye on the most. It's baked into her way of operating, regardless of context or life area.

Whether your primary myth feels more fluid or enduring, understanding what it is will help you spot the most common self-sabotaging pattern in your life right now and will give you the power to course-correct. The year I finished up the proposal for this book, I was approaching burnout as I juggled the podcast, writing, and coaching, piling more and more onto my plate. I refused to take breaks during work sessions and tried to squeeze in more work instead of sitting down to eat a meal. After weeks of the same thing, my body started giving me some warning signs— my eyes were heavy throughout the day, I was groggy, and I began experiencing headaches and digestive issues. Because I'm so intimately engaged in this work, I knew I'd been caught—again—by my primary myth, Perfection. I'd been here many times before, and I needed to slow way down.

It was a hard decision, but I emailed all my private coaching clients and told them I planned to take time off in December and January to replenish myself; it was important that I be vulnerable and own my truth. I gave them the option to stop or to continue coaching sessions with me in the new year, without pressuring them in any direction. I also backed out of any trips and gatherings I had previously agreed to go on, again telling people *why*: I was approaching burnout because of my unquenchable desire to achieve (for real!). Folks appreciated the brutal honesty.

That's the beauty of knowing and owning your primary myth— you can communicate it with directness and vulnerability to the other people in your life. Slowing down allowed me to recover and reapproach my service to women with fresh eyes and inspiration. When we are self-aware, we can be vigilant about our main self-sabotaging pattern, catch ourselves, and choose another direction.

The Assessment

Before we go deep into each Good Girl Myth, let's understand where you're standing right now. Take the following assessment to discover how truly deep and loud each myth is in your life. Circle the statement that most answers "I am more likely to . . ." You may find that both options apply; do your best to select the one that *most strongly* applies to you. You may also find that none of the options apply; do your best to select the one that most resonates with your past self or what others might say about you. If you really feel neither option applies, then skip the question, but do not skip more than five questions.

I am more likely to . . .	
1	**C**—Neglect my body throughout the day because I prioritize thinking and mental work **A**—Follow the norms of the community and culture I was born into (e.g., go to school, get a good job, get married)
2	**E**—Give up my time and energy to others as part of my role and sense of duty as mother, daughter, sister, partner, friend, or employee **C**—Touch my head and face a lot when I'm thinking
3	**E**—Feel depleted from supporting others or a cause I really believe in **B**—Criticize myself for my mistakes
4	**B**—Avoid taking action because I don't like making mistakes, being wrong, or looking stupid in front of others **E**—Help others even though they haven't asked for help
5	**E**—Think of myself last **D**—Keep the peace as much as I can
6	**A**—Avoid risky career moves like starting my own business or taking a sabbatical **B**—Approach burnout because I'm trying to excel in everything at once
7	**B**—Compete with others **C**—Distrust my feelings as irrational
8	**A**—Ask others for guidance and advice before checking in with myself **D**—Keep people around who bring me down
9	**B**—Avoid taking on challenges that I'm not good at solving right away **D**—Stay in problematic relationships longer than I need to
10	**B**—Have the feeling that what I'm doing is not enough **A**—Have trouble distinguishing between what I want to do with my life and what others expect of me

11	**E**—Lose sight of my purpose or goal because I'm busy helping others fulfill theirs **C**—Be skeptical of magic and unexplained phenomena
12	**A**—Trust others before myself **E**—Give a lot to others or to a greater mission
13	**D**—Avoid giving others feedback they need to hear **E**—Have trouble prioritizing my own self-care because I'm helping others or serving a greater cause
14	**D**—Undercommunicate my true feelings about a situation with others **B**—Try to overperform in all the roles of my life—wife, mother, career woman, and so on
15	**C**—Follow my head instead of my heart **D**—Make excuses for other people's bad behaviors
16	**A**—Dislike it when people don't follow the rules or an agreed-upon process **C**—Look at problems intellectually instead of emotionally
17	**B**—Hyperachieve in most, if not all, areas of life **A**—Feel I need more training and accreditation before I can do what I want to do
18	**B**—Resist making trade-offs and try to do as much as I can **C**—Choose practical career paths over more feeling-based, creative ones
19	**C**—Second-guess my first reaction and kick myself for it later **B**—Compare myself with others
20	**C**—Be conventionally smart, especially in areas that were highly rewarded in school, such as math, science, and languages (e.g., reading and writing) **D**—Gloss over what bothers me with a positive attitude

21	**D**—Bottle up my thoughts and opinions when I'm afraid they will anger or disappoint others **C**—Live my life "from the neck up" (i.e., in my head), disconnected from the rest of my body
22	**D**—Avoid confrontation and hard conversations **A**—Make specific plans so I know where I'm heading
23	**C**—Make decisions from a logical place, not so much an intuitive one **E**—Undervalue my time in comparison with other people's time
24	**C**—Overanalyze my decisions **A**—Do as I'm told
25	**D**—Make sure everybody gets along **B**—Give the impression that I do a lot without breaking a sweat
26	**E**—Feel that I'm responsible for helping fulfill others' needs and desires **A**—Follow rules whether they're being enforced or not
27	**D**—Tell people "I'm fine with it" when deep down I'm not **E**—Feel guilty about experiencing my own pleasure
28	**A**—Look for a formula or set of instructions **D**—Hold back what I'm really thinking and feeling so that I don't cause any problems in my relationships
29	**E**—Put other people's oxygen masks on before my own **B**—Avoid being or looking messy to the world
30	**A**—Wait or ask for permission before taking action **E**—Support others because I deeply empathize with their pain and challenges

Assessment Key

Rules = A   Perfection = B   Logic = C   Harmony = D   Sacrifice = E

Your Good Girl Score

Go through and count the number of times you circled each letter. Tally up your points below, and note any observations and insights you had during the assessment.

Letter	Good Girl Myth	Points	Observations
A	GGM #1: Rules		
B	GGM #2: Perfection		
C	GGM #3: Logic		
D	GGM #4: Harmony		
E	GGM #5: Sacrifice		
	Total		

Congrats! You've identified your good girl score. How do you feel about it? Was it surprising? Not surprising? Mind-bending? Heartbreaking? Soul spinning? Reaffirming? Tell me everything.

41

If you found that one myth didn't surface but two or three were tied, please don't sweat it. As you read through the chapters, your primary myth will come into focus.

If, after discovering your primary myth, you notice you're starting to feel bad about yourself, like there's something wrong with you or you have a deficit, I want to take a moment to give you a few reminders. First off, this *conditioning* is not your fault and can be unlearned. It's completely natural to have developed these tendencies having grown up in the patriarchy. Second, you are certainly not alone in experiencing your myths, as thousands of women can relate to you and grapple with the same struggles. No shame. We're in this together. Finally, don't forget that you are ultimately a powerful woman, and I'm supporting you in becoming even more powerful. Ultimately, seeing the ways you unconsciously sabotage yourself allows you to take more responsibility, instead of blaming what's "out there," and make more empowering choices.

Regardless of your primary myth, you'll want to journey with me through all the myths because all of them are within you (and certainly within the girls and women you know). Many of them are also incredibly intertwined, and they overlap and play off each other. Alas, we truly can't have one without the other. Of course, you'll want to take extra notes when we journey through *your* primary Good Girl Myth.

Our next stop? Why, the Myth of Rules, of course, which is by far the most invisible and sneaky and is the *key* to breaking the other four myths. Many good girl rule followers who take the assessment often don't score high for the Myth of Rules because it's the hardest myth to detect and admit to ourselves. So pack your bags, heroine, for the beast sleeps within.

4

The Myth of Rules

The Myth of Rules

SOUNDS LIKE

"If I follow the rules, life will be easier and I will get ahead."

LOOKS LIKE

The tendency to seek and follow external rules and authority instead of trusting our own desires, needs, and opinions.

MAIN STRATEGY FOR APPROVAL

Being good and following others' expectations.

POWERS YOU GIVE UP

Your purpose and self-authority.

I **FEEL LIKE MY HUSBAND AND I SHOULD BE TRYING FOR KIDS** by now," Jimena told me.

Whenever I hear a client say the word *should*, my ears perk up, and I tilt my head ever so slightly like my old shih tzu (RIP) used to do. I can tell the Myth of Rules lurks creepily nearby.

She continued, "My parents have been asking about it nonstop. His, too."

"Do you want kids?"

"I don't know. I definitely don't want to cause trouble with our families."

As we went on in the session, Jimena began deluding herself. Even though she *didn't know* whether she wanted kids, she felt she *should* have them. For generations, she told me, the women in her family have had at least three kids each. At least. How could she be the one to break the chain? It didn't feel right. It would be upsetting an entire tradition that needed to survive, especially according to her mom. Jimena, a high-level marketer at a top tech company, was almost thirty-seven years old. She had graduated from a top college, climbed up in her career, and made enough money to support herself, her husband, and her parents and even buy an apartment in the outskirts of the city. She had done everything right, except for the kids thing, because work had been too consuming. In fact, work was so overwhelming that slowing down to give herself the space to explore what she truly wanted seemed impossible to her. This train was moving fast, and she had been on it for almost two decades. When I brought up the possibility of taking a sabbatical from work to soul-search, rest, travel, and find alignment with her husband, she landed on me with another *should*:

"No, I should stay on track because I'm about to get promoted to VP," she said. "I've worked too hard for that."

"Do you want to be VP?"

"I think so," she said. Code words for "I don't know what I really want."

Toward the end of our session, she concluded, "I should keep working, and we'll also need to try conceiving this year," with zilch excitement.

"Jimena," I said. "In our session, you've said *should* at least seven or eight times. What does that tell us about how you *truly* feel?"

"I know," she said. "*Should* means obligation. I just feel all this pressure."

"Where do you feel this pressure?"

She crossed her arms over her chest and gripped her shoulders. "My upper back, my shoulders, my neck."

"You're carrying a lot," I said. "Many generations. Like you said."

"Exactly."

"Let me tell you about a nurse who studied her dying patients closely. What do you think she said was the number one regret most of them shared before they died?"

Jimena paused to contemplate. "That they should have said 'I love you' more?"

This is the part in the session where I lean forward, look my client in the eye, and drop a wisdom bomb I think she's ready to hear.

"No. The number *one* regret is that they lived a life that others expected of them and not one that was true to themselves."

I typically use wisdom bombs only when I really, really need to wake a client up. As with Jimena, who couldn't see that she was utterly and completely gripped by the Myth of Rules. This good girl programming was impacting every area of her life, from her mental well-being to her relationships with her husband, parents, and in-laws, to her decisions about her career and livelihood, to her decision about whether or not to have children and how she contributes her gifts to the world. She was blind to the fact that the Myth of Rules was leaking into every nook and cranny of her life, *insisting* she choose obligation and approval over her own desire and truth. And it was eating her alive.

If you want to live more powerfully and authentically, you must learn to question, break, bend, and even leverage the rules and expectations that exist within the major social systems, cultures, and traditions you were born into. You must learn to shed the reflexive and automatic *yes* of obedience. It's about taking back your power and listening to *your* unique heroine's journey—not anybody else's.

Why start with the Myth of Rules? Well, first, the Myth of Rules is the most invisible of all the Good Girl Myths because—as

I'll get to in a moment—from the time we're born, we're floating in millions of invisible rules. As one podcast listener told me, "I spent my marriage following my husband's rules for twenty years. But I didn't realize that's what I was doing. I was completely blind." Rules can be so hard to identify and detect that many of us begin to believe that they are actually our own ideas, choices, desires, and opinions. We've inherited them and bought into their empty promises. Let me put it this way: your life is an ocean, you're in a boat, and the society you grew up with has given you a map. You've been navigating your little boat by that map for years, and so you keep sailing in circles, missing the destination. Why? Because it isn't your map. The map doesn't emerge from your most authentic self.

The other reason to start here is that if you can't break the spell of the Myth of Rules, it will be difficult, maybe even impossible, to overcome your good girl programming. After all, the other four Good Girl Myths present their own types of power-sucking rules. Take the Myth of Harmony, for example. There lies the invisible rule that you should not speak up and you should value relationships over your own truth. Or, in the case of the Myth of Sacrifice, there lies the invisible rule that you should put others before yourself, even if it means sacrificing your fulfillment and well-being. In other words, the ability to question and break rules is the underlying superpower needed for everything else. It's the foundation.

Every day, I meet women who long to live more authentic and aligned lives but are so locked under the spell of the Myth of Rules that they continue on the expected, conventional, and safe path that pleases both their parents and their online bios. How come so many of us follow the rules? Because rules make the following three promises:

1. **If I follow the rules, I'll gain approval, connection, and even a sense of belongingness.**

    When we follow rules, especially those upheld and followed by the groups and people we respect in our lives, we receive approval. As humans, we have a fundamental need to belong, which is why the Myth of Rules works so powerfully—it cripples us on this level. It tells us if we don't follow the rules, we'll be banned from our tribe.

2. **If I follow the rules, I'll be in control, gaining ultimate safety and comfort.**

    Humans also have a fundamental need to be safe, and we often desire comfort over all things. One way we like to gain safety and comfort is by gaining control. Rules are straightforward and give us the illusion of being in control. They give us a specific formula and path to follow so we won't risk any mistakes, detours, or waywardness.

3. **If I follow the rules, I'll experience more convenience and ease.**

    Humans love convenience. Since rules are simple and provide clarity, they can save us a ton of energy and cut back on the cognitive load of making decisions. With rules, we don't have to think for ourselves, or at all, for that matter! We can simply go along with the program. They provide that easy shortcut.

Even if rules give us these benefits, the cost is much higher. When you seek approval, you give up your own desires and even the possibility to *know* what you desire. We may end up belonging to a tribe, but we are banished from ourselves—we lose connection with our most authentic selves. When you seek safety and comfort, you give up growth and expansion. Your fear of making mistakes or the wrong decision puts you in a passive, go-along-with-life state instead of making you the heroine of your own story. When you seek convenience, you give up the beauty of sponta-neity, flow, and creativity that emerges from not having an easy and efficient plan, from saying yes to a perhaps longer and slower but more fulfilling road, from sensing the way forward instead of assuming it's already been laid out for you and all you have to do is follow it. Your desire for a formula stifles your unique expression, which the world is hungry for.

In the end, when you follow the Myth of Rules, you don't even explore or become in touch with your authentic gifts—that expres-sion is not even possible. And, at its most threatening, the Myth of Rules prevents us from sharing our true gifts. By *gifts*, I don't mean only our talents and skills; I mean our *offerings*—what it is that we want to give to the world that will make a difference, big or small. And note: our true gifts can exist within or outside our careers.

So yes, the Myth of Rules is dangerous. It makes us delay our dreams and look to others, instead of ourselves, to tell us what to do. It also keeps us policing ourselves, convincing ourselves that "we couldn't possibly," or that our dream or idea is simply "ridic-ulous," and that we'd better keep dancing to the same old beat of society's drum. It forces us to wait for someone else to give us the green light, discover us, and recognize us for our hard work. It tells us we're not "expert enough" because we keep defining expertise the way a specific industry or system does. The Myth of Rules keeps us in our schoolgirl days, when we waited on our parents and teachers for guidance.

When we break the Myth of Rules, we reclaim our self-authority. We become clear about what gives our lives meaning.

We redefine success for ourselves, outside the scope of any systems we were born into. We learn to do the most vital thing for our growth—take risks and step into the wild unknown. Worth it, if you ask me.

Invisible Rules

There are two kinds of rules in the world: visible and invisible. Most of us can easily identify visible rules—they're easy to spot. These rules are as loud as stop signs and traffic lights. They're the rules and laws that are spelled out, codified, written down, and agreed upon. Breaking visible rules has physical, legal, or financial consequences. If you don't show up to work for weeks, you'll be fired. If you don't show up to court, you will be arrested.

Then there is the second category of rules, and these are the ones I want us to focus on—invisible rules. Few of us have taken the time or energy to question the invisible rules that surround and trap us. Invisible rules tiptoe around us, like masked thieves, right past our alarm systems. These are the rules that are not discussed or consciously agreed upon but exist simply because we live in a certain culture or system. Invisible rules are the messages we receive about how we should be or behave. Here's the thing: invisible rules are inevitable. When humans get together in groups, they create and follow what social psychologists call *norms* to help them know how to behave, make decisions, and avoid conflict. Remember the third promise that rules provide? Norms provide us with those convenient mental shortcuts and social scripts. Take a moment to reflect on that. How many groups are you a part of? Each group has thousands of norms you follow. And the truth is, norms can be super helpful. For example, during college, I co-facilitated a support group made up of survivors of sexual assault. While we had a bunch of visible rules that we agreed upon together to help create psychological safety (e.g., don't provide feedback on people's assault experiences), there were also thousands of invisible rules we implicitly agreed to simply by being in the group. If someone had brought a book to read silently while other members shared, that would have felt terrible! We didn't have a specific, visible rule around it, but we did have an invisible one: give people your full attention.

When are invisible rules dangerous? When they conflict with our true values and desires but, because we can't see them (which means they largely operate within our subconscious), we don't even realize we're going along with the program. If shame and fear are used as tools to enforce norms, then these norms are unhealthy. If individuals experience extreme punishment or backlash for questioning norms, then again, they're unhealthy. Period.

Invisible rules can also be dangerous if they were once useful in our childhood (e.g., "Always listen to your parents") but have now expired. As children, we were kept safe by these rules as our brains, bodies, and understanding of the world were still developing. But as adults, we are actually stifled and suffocated by these same rules without our realizing it. If you don't have your own compass to live by, you'll naturally default to the rules you learned to tell you what to do and who to be.

The point is, every single rule in this world was created by an individual, group, or organization. The rules are 100 percent socially fabricated. In chapter 2, I shared how the patriarchy infiltrates us through four main spheres of influence during our early years: our families, schools, and religions and the larger, mainstream pop culture we consume. Well, the easiest way for the patriarchy to do this is by codifying and upholding rules.

So it's essential to opt in to invisible rules with our eyes wide open. But sadly, most of us inherit the invisible rules from these spheres of influence without a second thought, and they stay with us for the rest of our lives. Do you think you're aware of the invisible rules you're following? How can you break free from a cage you don't even see? First you must *see* the cage. Let's get to know which invisible rules you may be unknowingly following by taking the time to look at each of these systems. Shall we?

Our Families

If you've ever watched a baby in a high chair, you know babies love throwing things on the floor! They take that spoonful of baby food and hurl it over the edge, watching as it falls to see what happens. They're doing what babies are supposed to do, which is to learn about the world around them through their senses. Babies certainly don't do the most civilized, clean, or convenient thing. They do what feels good and natural in their bodies. Through the natural process of socialization, our parents or legal guardians are the first people to give us rules—they tell us where and how to eat, where and how to go to the bathroom, and where and how to use our crayons and markers (not on the walls but on paper, for example).

Babies can't get away with being free-spirited creative messes for too long, especially not girls. There was a study that looked at how parents teach their kids how to go down a firehouse-type pole in a free-play session. Girls were given more explanations and physical assistance than boys, even though there were no differences in the kids' playground chops or ability to slide down a pole![1] By

FAMILY RULES CHECKLIST

What are some of the invisible rules I internalized from my family?

Check all boxes that apply.

☐ I should stay at home.

☐ I should cook and clean.

☐ I should not disappoint or upset my parents.

☐ I should take care of my siblings and/or others.

☐ I should earn a good salary.

☐ I should work in the workplace.

☐ I should be self-employed and start my own business.

☐ I should choose a safe and conventional career.

☐ I should marry.

☐ I should have children.

☐ I should be a good mother.

☐ Other _____

doubting girls and hovering over them to make sure they don't fall, parents teach their daughters to doubt themselves. And when we doubt ourselves, we lose our self-authority and are more likely to turn to rules and to the powers that be to give us the answers.

Rules, like authority figures, give us clear guidelines about what to do and what not to do. Instead of trusting what *feels* good and taking a risk (like throwing the spoon on the floor to see what happens or sliding down that fire pole), we look for something external to show us the way. We trust authorities and rules more and trust ourselves, and our natural curiosity, less.

We also hear these rules in our grandparents' and extended family's traditions and customs. "Ahh, one day you're going to have beautiful babies," said one of my great-aunties in Argentina, pinching my cheeks, after my husband, Enrique, and I married. "Maybe," I thought. "Maybe."

Our Schools

Our teachers and schools also have a list of rules they require us to follow. Schools have rules about attendance, performance, safety, you name it. Three hundred sixty studies conducted in thirty countries have shown that girls consistently outperform boys in school.[2] It's not because we're smarter; it's because we follow rules, and the school system is set up to reward the rule followers.

 EDUCATION RULES CHECKLIST

What are some of the invisible rules I internalized from my schools?
Check all boxes that apply.

☐ I should be the best in my grade.

☐ I should win the contest(s).

☐ I should be harder working than other students.

☐ I should get good grades.

☐ I should get good feedback from teachers.

☐ I should not disappoint or upset my teachers.

☐ I should follow the rubric and template.

☐ I should participate in competitive sports.

☐ I should value mathematics/sciences over arts.

- ☐ I should get into the best possible college.
- ☐ I should be special, be above average, and stand out.
- ☐ I should excel in all areas of learning (straight As).
- ☐ I should earn a graduate degree or the highest degree possible.
- ☐ Other _____

We raise our hand to speak, turn in our homework on time, and seldom skip class. We're good girls.

Our Religions

Religions are systems with a lot of freakin' rules. These rules affect us down the line, even in our professional lives. Take Agatha, a twenty-six-year-old woman who was engaged to an engineer and lived in a chic apartment in an up-and-coming part of San Francisco. We started working together because as a first-time manager at her job, she was nervous and anxious pretty much twenty-four seven. Every time she made a decision at work, she would run and tell her boss. "I want him to tell me I'm doing the right thing. It's almost like I'm . . . confessing," she whispered. Agatha grew up in an ultra-Catholic household, surrounded by clear, dominant authority figures (e.g., her mother, her stepdad, the local church's priest) who told her *exactly* what to do her entire life. Between the ages of nine and sixteen, she went to confession every single week. That's a ton of confessions for a sweet, innocent little pea, don't you think? I asked her to tell me what kinds of things she would confess. "I had this notebook," she said, "and I would write down all the things I did wrong that week to bring to

RELIGIOUS RULES CHECKLIST

What are some of the invisible rules I internalized from my religion?

Check all boxes that apply.

☐ I should be sexually conservative.

☐ I should be a virgin before marriage.

☐ I should be self-sacrificing.

☐ I should be service-minded.

☐ I should feel guilty.

☐ I should not be bad or sin.

☐ I should feel responsible and beg for forgiveness.

☐ I should look and feel modest.

☐ I should believe in a more powerful God.

☐ I should obey the holders of knowledge (often male), such as priests, rabbis, and gurus.

☐ I should go to church/mass/synagogue/mosque.

☐ I should believe in scripture without question.

☐ I should believe my religion's way is the best or only way to God.

☐ Other _____

confession. It was silly. Like shopping on a Sunday, the Sabbath, instead of during the week." (If you're thinking "All I want to do is take Agatha out shopping on Sundays," you're not alone.) Rules gave Agatha comfort and security because she didn't have to risk being wrong or getting in trouble, plus she simply wasn't used to making her own.

At the end of the day, religion is based on external authorities and rules that tell us what we should and shouldn't be doing in order to be pure and gain access to an afterlife or Heaven. One of the biggest rules religion places on girls and women regards their sexuality. Many different religions insist girls be unrealistically pure in thought and action, which causes them to dangerously internalize shame and develop post-traumatic stress disorder when they experience any ounce of natural sexual desire. In such religions, girls are expected to "take on the burden" and behave and dress modestly to make sure they're not too attractive to men (who apparently can't control themselves). Religion and the Myth of Rules make a wonderful, powerful duo here.

Pop Culture

Although we grow up in different families, schools, and religions, we're all absorbing the similar expectations and norms of a larger Western mainstream pop culture, such as television, news, film, magazines, and music. From Disney, I learned that I should wait for a prince to take care of me and that it's best to wait for good fortune to come to me instead of going after it. From horror movies, I learned that I should be sexually prudish, since it's the sexually active girls who are killed first. From romance movies, I learned I should help bad boys become good. From Britney Spears, Lindsay Lohan, and Paris Hilton, I learned it was cool and even attractive to get wasted in public. From the Kardashians, I learned I should be "slim thick" (you know, itty-bitty waist but still curvy). And the list goes on and on. We're bombarded with messages about how to behave and act from the larger culture we live in.

POP CULTURE RULES CHECKLIST

What are some of the invisible rules I internalized from the larger culture, such as television, film, and music?
Check all boxes that apply.

☐ I should consume television, film, and music.

☐ I should know what's going on in the news.

☐ I should follow and admire celebrities and models.

☐ I should follow fashion trends.

☐ I should find my "soul mate" and be monogamous.

☐ I should be beautiful, which means looking young, thin, and free of body hair.

☐ I should buy products that help me attain a certain beauty standard.

☐ I should buy products in general to make me feel better.

☐ I should like bad boys who treat me poorly.

☐ I should show my skin and be revealing.

☐ I should be sexually experienced and skilled.

☐ I should have a big social media following.

☐ Other _____

Go Deeper and Learn More About Yourself

Where do most of your invisible rules come from? On the preceding lists, look at where you have the most check marks, or notice which system feels the most charged for you. Some of us grew up in nonreligious families, for example, but were expected to perform very well in school. Some of us may not have paid as much attention to school but grew up modeling or competing in sports, with a lot of pressure on how to look and act a certain way.

Did you have check marks all the way down? Don't be discouraged. Awareness is the first step to deconditioning. Or you may have already been aware of these rules, but now you have them in front of you, where you can see them and point to them.

Did you notice any contradictions? For example, "I should stay at home" and "I should work in the workplace" might be two rules that you've internalized. Because we live under multiple systems at the same time, it's natural that invisible rules contradict each other. The result is that we often feel confused, but neither of the rules is emerging from our authentic selves.

Did you find it hard to question some of your invisible rules? You might be thinking, "Is it so bad that I want to be a good mother, or that I wanted to be a good student, or that I want to be a good person? Don't we want good mothers, students, and people in our society?" Yes. Definitely. But here's the issue: (1) *we* haven't defined for *ourselves* what is good—instead, we're born into these systems that define it for us; (2) these expectations of goodness become pressures that lead us to never feeling good enough (as we'll see in the Myth of Perfection); and (3) there's very little room for mistakes and imperfections, which ultimately lead to feelings of guilt and shame. For these reasons, it's super important that we question the invisible rules in our lives, no matter how well-intentioned they seem on the surface.

The Four Pathway Reframes

Once we become aware of our invisible rules, we can begin to think about the big picture—our destiny. After all, rules impact our small, daily actions, and those actions make up our lives. As good girls operating under this myth, we're thinking too narrowly about our path and destiny. This is where our design thinking–inspired mind-sets come in. Let's look at our second mind-set, *open your mind*. When using design thinking, one of the ways we open our minds is by reframing problems. Reframing is about looking at a problem in a fresh, new (and sometimes opposite) way, freeing up our energy and ability to take action. One of my clients was feeling shame because she had been divorced twice before the age of forty. According to her, the problem was simple: She was a failure when it came to marriage. Oh, and people aren't trustworthy. Through coaching, we tried on a few reframes to see what felt best. What if we believed that she "failed fast" at marriages so that she could quickly learn what doesn't work and share those lessons with others? What if her feelings of failure in this area were the catalyst that led her to finally write that book of poetry? What if we reframed categorizing her latest ex-wife from "terrible human" to a key character who played a specific role, that is, luring my client to New York, where she could fulfill her destiny as an artist? As we played with these reframes, she felt empowered, creatively inspired, and even grateful—a stark contrast to her initial feelings of shame, failure, and mistrust. It really is about the story we choose to tell ourselves, isn't it? Let's reframe four of the core dysfunctional beliefs sitting right beneath the Myth of Rules.

61

Reframe #1

MYTH OF RULES: I have a paved path or destiny waiting to be discovered (passive).

REFRAME: There is no paved path. I make my path while and by walking forward into the unknown. I codesign my destiny with the Universe (active, therefore empowering).

Poet Antonio Machado once wrote, "By walking one makes the road, and upon glancing behind one sees the path that never will be trod again. Wanderer, there is no road—Only wakes upon the sea." I love this image of "wakes upon the sea." The sea is a metaphor for the unknown, the great mystery that is our future. When we're under the Myth of Rules, we're looking for that rubric, formula, or set of instructions to tell us how to proceed. But there is no set of instructions for your essential self, for your soul. Roz Savage spent eleven years as a management consultant, feeling utterly unfulfilled, before she decided to row herself *sola* across the Atlantic Ocean. I'll share more about Roz later, but at first glance it's easy to think she was "destined" to follow that calling and that one day she had an "epiphany" that revealed that specific destiny to her. But is that the whole truth? No. Roz actively *chose* her destiny, when she could have chosen many others.

You make your path as much as you listen for it. Just as the best design relies on radical collaboration, we radically codesign our lives with the Universe. You must actively engage with your options and course-correct as you go. You can no longer be told what to do or wait for permission. You blaze the path by walking it. There's no rubric, map, formula, or rule book. Sure, you can have jumping-off points and be inspired by others' journeys, but at the end of the day there are no rules or wrong turns, only the vast ocean for you to navigate in your own glorious way.

"The marvelous thing about going through life with the intention of writing a story about it later," Roz told me, "is that we make ourselves the heroines of our own story. It allows a degree of detachment from it, so we mind less how happy and secure we feel in the moment; we start seeking out experiences that will be exciting and transformative *because* it's going to make a better story. I think that's the whole idea behind the heroine's journey. Imagine we could all start really living our lives from that place of thinking, 'How can I make my life as epic a story as I possibly can?'"[3]

Roz *decided* to row herself across the ocean because she knew it would make a better story and therefore catch people's attention about ocean pollution.

You write your story. You design your path. No more waiting.

Reframe #2

MYTH OF RULES: There is a right path and a wrong path.

REFRAME: All paths are fine, so I'll keep on walking.

Let's let go of the ridiculous idea that there is a right path to choose. Too many of us good girls are obsessed with overthinking and feel stuck in or disengaged with our lives because we're afraid of choosing the wrong path. We're afraid one choice could be the be-all and end-all. In design thinking, we have a saying: "Don't be precious." *Don't be precious* is exactly as it sounds. People get attached to their ideas like Gollum in *Lord of the Rings* and whisper "My precious" over them as if the fate of Middle Earth depended on it, when ideas are a dime a dozen and what matters more is whether and how you bring them into reality.[4] But it applies to our lives too, so you'll hear me bring it up a lot. Don't be too precious about anything, not even your career path (yes, you can quote me on it).

In an even deeper sense, can you ever truly know which turn you take is right or wrong? Take a look at this Taoist proverb:

> *There was a farmer whose horse ran away. That evening the neighbors gathered to commiserate with him since this was such bad luck. He said, "May be." The next day the horse returned, but brought with it six wild horses, and the neighbors came exclaiming at his good fortune. He said, "May be." And then, the following day, his son tried to saddle and ride one of the wild horses, was thrown, and broke his leg. Again the neighbors came to offer their sympathy for the misfortune. He said, "May be." The day after that, conscription officers came to the village to seize young men for the army, but because of the broken leg the farmer's son was rejected. When the neighbors came in to say how fortunately everything had turned out, he said, "May be."[5]*

In some translations of the story, the farmer answers, "Is it good or bad?" Only time reveals what's good or bad, which is why it's much easier to connect the dots when looking back and impossible to do when looking forward. Some seemingly good things bring bad results and vice versa, which goes on forever, so it doesn't make sense to praise or criticize them in the moment because we don't really know. This farmer was at peace with not knowing whether the events happening to him were good or bad, and we can learn from that. The Myth of Rules has brainwashed us into thinking there is a right or wrong path, but there isn't—there is only *your* path, made by walking, so don't let your attachment to the "right" path block movement and energy. Keep moving.

Reframe #3

MYTH OF RULES: I should follow one path and stay consistent.

REFRAME: I can follow multiple paths because I'm multidimensional and evolving.

The Myth of Rules sold you a lie: *you should have one main (cookie-cutter) career path.* And *don't forget to retire early!* The Myth of Rules keeps putting us in boxes, labels, roles, norms, and titles, instead of embracing the magical multidimensionality of our being. Walt Whitman famously wrote in his epic poem *Song of Myself,* "I am large, I contain multitudes."[6] As do you, heroine.

I once did a training with an older female author I deeply admire. During a late-night private conversation, she pointed at the purple cloth around her wrist, saying, "This is purple. We can put it in that category. But it's also elastic. It's also soft. It's also many things. It has many properties. If we say it's only 'purple,' we miss so many other things. You're the same way." As she kept reminding us, "By thirty years of age, you already have thirty selves inside of you!" Self is multiple. Self changes and is fluid. Self is adaptable. Self has contradictions. You can be highly multi- and interdisciplinary. You can cross borders and bridges. You can get creative and evolve. We often expect people to be static, fixed, and consistent in their careers, but we have far too many selves and parts within us that make choosing feel like an anxiety-filled process. In recent years, the self-help industry has jumped on the bandwagon, telling us we must find our *one* passion, *one* calling, *one* destiny. Whoa, that's a lot of pressure. It ain't so. You have multiple callings because you have multiple selves. As we'll soon see, design thinking can provide us with tools for exploring these multiple pathways.

Reframe #4

MYTH OF RULES: I need more experience before I walk my path.

REFRAME: I can walk my path with the experience I have *right now*.

Let's talk about expertise. Many of us good girls withhold permission from ourselves because we believe we aren't an expert or experienced enough in the pathways we want to pursue. Our culture is obsessed with expertise (and specialization), and far too many of us are brainwashed by this old-fashioned thinking that we must keep consuming information and training before we can share our gifts.

Here's a radical idea. You don't receive your expertise from the outside; *you* integrate and create it from where you're standing right now. The word *expert* comes from the Latin *expertus*, which means "tried." An expert is someone who has tried. Expertise comes from your unique, direct experience. It certainly doesn't come from other people. Yet we're constantly looking to others, people who often have *less* relevant experience than we do, to give us the answers. During my podcast interview with bestselling author and psychotherapist Esther Perel, she shared how our culture urges people to "consume expertise" by constantly making them feel inept. "Let me listen to you," she shared, referring to her audience. "And help you see how much *you* know that you don't think you know because you're doubting yourself. . . . That's a whole different way of dealing with empowerment."[7]

Do not erase your past; leverage it and share the colorful tapestry of who you are. We are tired of flat, straightforward, cookie-cutter, boring same-same. *Don't* hide your complexity.

And don't buy into the Myth of Rules's lie that expertise comes from the accreditation of a specific system, industry, or senior expert. Sure it can, but it's not the *only* place. Expertise (and therefore your permission) comes from a myriad of places—your desires, values, skills, and roots and your story, to name a few. In fact, when you think about differentiation and what makes you unique, it isn't another title or degree that millions of others also earn. It's the *details* of who you are. Your originality and authenticity come from those details. You're the designer of your life, so you can broaden your expertise to include *all* of who you are. You can even do away with this concept of expertise altogether if you choose.

Caveat: I'm not saying skills development and rigorous training (e.g., for becoming a neurosurgeon) can simply be thrown out the window. I'm saying get the baseline training you need and move on. Don't get stuck in perpetual preparation, going after more degrees, taking countless seminars, reading book after book after book, instead of actually sharing your gifts and making a difference. Ask yourself, *Do I really need that training, or can I start from where I am now? What am I afraid of if I start from where I am now?* If you're afraid of making mistakes or getting in trouble or you are thinking "I couldn't . . . ," then you're still gripped by your good girl conditioning.

Redefine Success

If we want to design a life and career that brings us deep satisfaction, meaning is the foundation. It starts from inside out, not outside in. One of our core mind-sets inspired by design thinking is to seek deeper understanding through empathy. As you might recall from the first chapter, in the empathy phase, a designer puts herself in the users' shoes to understand their needs and desires. Like an anthropologist, she uses field observations and in-depth interviews. In the next few pages, we're going to be our own designers, and our project is our life, interviewing ourselves so that we can unearth what I call our "ingredients of meaning." We'll later use these ingredients to brainstorm more possibilities for our lives. Ready?

The Wisdom of Joy

The first ingredient of meaning is joy. My client Kristi's parents circled in high society, frequented the big old country clubs, and had big expectations for their daughter. In one of our sessions, she confessed that she was still clinging to one of those rules she learned in childhood, telling me, "I'm creating false pressure of what I should be doing based on what I think my parents want me to do." Kristi came to me because she was between jobs and had no idea what she wanted to do next. She had worked as a project manager at a design agency and then bridged into interaction design. Throughout that journey, she had completely forgotten what truly mattered to her, so we needed to rediscover her meaning. We did that by answering the following questions:

WHAT BRINGS YOU JOY?

Identify three activities that you intrinsically enjoy.

_____

_____

_____

1. What feels good?

Growing up, Kristi would wake up at five o'clock each morning to practice tennis. By the time she was an adult, playing tennis had become a very routinized activity that felt like an obligation. When she was a little girl, however, before all the structure and competition, tennis was a source of play and adventure. She could play for hours. It wasn't until playing tennis became something she had to do, a rule book she had to follow, that she lost her joy in it.

The Myth of Rules (along with the Myth of Perfection) can suck the joy out of some of our greatest sources of natural, intrinsic joy and pleasure, which is dangerous because enjoyment and attention are interrelated. Schoolteachers know this best—when students don't enjoy something, they're less likely to stay engaged with it.

Close your eyes and ask yourself a simple question: *What gives me joy?* And if you can't conjure anything up right now, throw yourself back to girlhood: What *gave* me joy? Joy was something we felt in the body. When Kristi touched on her joy, her eyes would brim with tears, and she would get a feeling of being choked up with emotion. How does joy feel in your body? In Sanskrit there's a word, *ananda*, which means bliss and extreme delight. As Joseph Campbell once said in a PBS interview with Bill Moyers, "Where is your bliss station?"

2. What sustains your attention?

When searching for meaning, a good place to start is to follow your attention. We've all experienced that Zen-like state of mind that hooks us for hours on end. This state goes by many names, whether it's *rapture, bliss, the zone, the groove,* or *flow.* Positive psychologist Mihaly Csikszentmihalyi coined the theory of flow when he first observed surfers who would go out in the early morning to catch waves for hours. In an interview with *Wired* magazine, Csikszentmihalyi described flow as "being completely involved in an activity for its own sake. The ego falls away. Time flies. Every action, movement, and thought follows inevitably from the previous one, like playing jazz. Your whole being is involved, and you're using your skills to the utmost."[8]

When Kristi and I looked at where she was most absorbed in her life, experiencing long states of flow, it became obvious that she was in a state of bliss whenever she was working on an art or design project. As she described to me once, "My brain is working, but I'm not thinking. I am letting my hands and eyes do the thinking and problem solving."

That's exactly it: flow happens when you hit that sweet spot between your level of challenge and your level of skill. If your skill is too high, you'll get bored. If the activity is too challenging, you'll get anxious. I know that when I enter states of flow with writing, for example, hours will go by and I'll have completely lost track of time and, sometimes, my sense of place in space and time. That's flow. It's when you merge with the activity, lose yourself, and feel that oneness. Work can feel sacred and be one of the most meaningful aspects of being human. So I'll ask you again: What absorbs you? Write down your top three activities. The answer to that question will give you a big clue about the work that's most meaningful to you.

IDENTIFY YOUR FLOW

Identify at least three activities that put you in a state of flow.

_____

_____

_____

3. What are you curious about?

In *Big Magic*, Liz Gilbert talks about following your curiosity, more so than your passion. When you think about it, curiosity is about what *first* captures your attention. It also helps surface certain subjects or threads to our attention again and again. I like to tell my clients that curiosity can feel like something or someone knocking on their door, begging them to open it. It'll just keep knocking. So don't dismiss the strange questions that pop into your head as distracting or ridiculous ideas or hobbies; they might lead you somewhere interesting. They might lead you to your new career pathway. They might balance out an intense job.

Kristi grew up doodling in the margins of her notebooks, and because of this, she became curious about lettering. This curiosity led her to enroll in a workshop on printmaking while vacationing with her husband in Berlin. She came home and experimented with doing custom hand-lettering on different materials, such as thank-you cards, and even started teaching her own printmaking workshops. Today Kristi is a letterer, in addition to a product design consultant. Creativity doesn't have to come in lightning strikes, says Gilbert; it can come in "whispers."[9] I love that: curiosity speaks in whispers, so all you have to do is lean in and listen and be open to where it leads you.

WHAT'S WHISPERING TO YOU?

Identify three things you're curious about.

_____

_____

_____

Have you answered these three questions—what feels good, what sustains your attention, and what you are curious about? If so, you're off to a good start. But the flip side of joy is pain and suffering, the second ingredient of meaning, which we'll dive into next.

The Wisdom of Pain

Pain is a powerful teacher. Some of our greatest gifts come from our deepest challenges. I once coached a woman who worked for a venture capital firm and felt that her career was meaningless. She was also a sexual assault survivor, and through our work together she realized that she had a great opportunity to support other sexual assault survivors. She went on to become a social worker who supports women in cases of domestic and sexual abuse.

As author Isabel Allende once told me, "I think going through the darkness is a time when we bring out from inside of us the strength that we don't even know we have. So the heroine becomes a heroine *after* going through the trials, not before. No one is born a heroine. What makes a heroine is the trials." So, heroine, let me see your scar badge.

 JOURNALING ABOUT CHALLENGES

Grab your journal and freewrite responses to the following questions.

- What have been your greatest life challenges? These can be moments of conflict or trauma.

- Where have you learned the greatest lessons about yourself and the world?

- What frustrates you? What problem do you care to solve for yourself and/or others?

- What are some personal beliefs, thoughts, or ideas you've held about the world and/or yourself that have disconnected you from a more authentic version of yourself? "I used to believe ... and then I discovered ..."

- What are some of the cultural, social, and educational systems that have disconnected you from a more authentic version of yourself?

- What are some of the struggles your family, culture, and/or peer group have undergone that really stand out to you?

It's important that during this exercise you reserve any judgment of your challenges. Even if your challenges seem small compared with, say, world hunger, they're still important. And if you've been through lots of challenging situations, tread lightly and be gentle on yourself.

The Wisdom of Death

Remember Roz, our fellow heroine who rowed herself across three oceans? Before she took the leap, she felt like she had been "faking it for over a decade" at her management consultant job, a dissatisfaction that led her to read a ton of self-help books and stumble across a brief journaling exercise (see, those can work!). The exercise involved taking ten minutes out of her day to write two versions of her obituary. The first version was her life if she didn't have any constraints or doubts, and the second version was her life if she carried on living the way she was living—the one under the Myth of Rules. It was powerful and shocking for her to see the stark difference. She reflected, "My objective became much more about living life vividly and vigorously rather than safely." Roz was *not* a lifelong Division 1 rower; she wasn't even particularly adventurous or sporty until this point. Wrap your mind around that for a moment: *this five-foot-four woman rowed herself across the entire Atlantic Ocean.* She went on to row across the Pacific and Indian Oceans as well.

Death is not only the great equalizer—we all die—but also the great clarifier: How do you want to live and how do you want to be? As Steve Jobs famously said in his 2005 Stanford commencement speech, "Remembering that I'll be dead soon is the most important tool I've ever encountered to help me make the big choices in life. Because almost everything—all external expectations, all pride, all fear of embarrassment or failure—these things just fall away in the face of death, leaving only what is truly important." Looking at what we can learn from the perspective death brings to our lives is the third ingredient in finding meaning in our lives.

 WHAT WOULD YOU REGRET?

Identify three things you would regret not doing if you died in five years.

_____

_____

_____

Unfortunately, since death is taboo in our society, people don't like to cozy up to it, even in a safe, hypothetical way. But spiritual traditions have been working with death meditations and visualizations for millennia. In fact, imagining your last years, months, weeks, days, and hours on the Earth helps you cut straight to what matters most. So, are you ready to inch a bit closer to death, even for a few brief moments? It's okay if you don't feel ready; remember, heroine, discomfort equals growth.

 DEATH MEDITATION

Cozy up to death to see what it reveals for you by experiencing my free Death Meditation, which you can find on my website: majomeditation.com.

Imagine New Possibilities

By paying attention to your joy and suffering and reflecting on your life from the perspective of death, you've collected your ingredients of meaning. Congrats! You now have a hatful of things that really matter to you, some that seem connected and some that, at first glance, seem completely unrelated. Maybe you received a major insight, or maybe you're more confused. Either way, all is well.

Now it's time to *open your mind*, broaden your range of possibilities, and break free from the Myth of Rules, which has us in a rigid, one-size-fits-all (boring) track. One of the more interesting phenomena I've discovered in my coaching—even in coaching creatives—is that it's very hard for us to be creative about our own lives. Under the Myth of Rules, we limit ourselves and say things like "I couldn't possibly get away with that" or "That's too crazy." We're happy to be creative for *others* or on paper, but when it comes to thinking about our own lives, we consider only a handful of options. One of the best ways to open our minds is through brainstorming.

Brainstorming may be an activity you've heard a lot about, one that might even make you roll your eyes. But it's an art and a skill many of us have no clue how to actually do. In fact, I'd say many of us *think* we're brainstorming (yes, you too, designers) when we're only scratching the surface of an actual brainstorm. Brainstorming is generating as many new ideas as possible in a given amount of time. It's a form of *divergent thinking*, which is when we purposefully flare out and think outside of our normal frames and lenses. While *convergent thinking* asks us to hone in and focus on a particular idea, divergent thinking is the opposite—it's all about generating new ideas outward. In brainstorming there are no stupid ideas—you want to go for weird, interesting things that make no sense in order to open up what's possible for you; that's how breakthroughs and shifts happen. Here are guidelines for brainstorming outlined in designer Tom Kelley's book *The Ten Faces of Innovation* (commentary is mine):[10]

1. Go for quantity.

To get to really good ideas, you need to generate a huge number of them. First ideas aren't usually good, and only a small percentage are actually interesting, so cast a wide net.

2. Encourage wild ideas.

Wild ideas are how you get to innovative solutions. Don't be afraid to suggest weird and funky ideas.

3. Be visual.

Pick up a marker pen and represent your ideas with quick sketches and figures.

4. Defer judgment.

This applies to other people's ideas as well as your own. Using techniques from improv, say "Yes, and . . ." and build on other people's ideas. This means you'll have to suspend your inner critic.

5. One conversation at a time.

Don't talk over each other if you're doing this in a group setting. (In fact, brainstorming is often most effective when done alone and ideas are shared in a group afterward.)[11]

Using your ingredients of meaning that we discovered together, you're ready to brainstorm! Use the following exercise.

 BRAINSTORM AROUND MEANING

At the d.school, we start brainstorms with "How might we . . . ?" In your case, pick an ingredient of meaning—it doesn't matter which one—and ask yourself "How might I . . . ?" For example, *How might I support low-income students with their homework?*

Grab a marker and a bunch of sticky notes and set a timer for five minutes. For each idea, start your answer with "What if . . ." Answering with "What if . . ." will allow you to stay open and imaginative and will build excitement. For example, *What if I started a tutoring company? What if I matched YMCA spaces with after-school homework periods? What if I made a theater company that rewards kids for doing their homework with live shows? What if? What if? What if?* One idea per sticky note. Remember, it's okay if your ideas are outlandish, dumb, or nonsensical, as you're stretching for quantity and trying to bypass your inner critic through speed and not overthinking.

In the next chapter, we'll learn how we can begin to implement ideas in small, friendly ways, so make sure you can reference your sticky notes later.

Brainstorm Through Blending

Often it can be difficult to choose just one ingredient, so I like to slightly constrain brainstorms by blending two or more ingredients together. After all, creativity (our sweet antidote to rules) is a process of mixing and blending. Artists mix pigments to create millions of colors. Designers blend materials and experiences to make millions of products and services. Alchemists mix elixirs to create new metals. Blending, integrating, connecting, mixing—that's *how* the magic happens. At the intersection of two materials or ideas, new worlds we never thought possible suddenly emerge.

So, what does blending look like? Let's circle back to my multi-passionate client Kristi. Before she landed on lettering as a major focus, we uncovered a ton of other ingredients of meaning (chocolate making, interaction design, cooking, crafting, event planning, research, storytelling, and the list went on). Kristi was feeling overwhelmed. "How do I choose?" she asked.

"Let's get creative," I said. "How might we blend, combine, and intersect them?"

"Combine these interests?" She stared at the stickies strewn over the marble coffee table.

"Yeah, let's start with statements of 'What if . . . ?,' such as 'What if I . . . ?' And remember, in brainstorming we have the mind-set of 'Yes, and . . . ,' to build off each other."

She paused and looked up at the ceiling. "Okay. What if I designed an app for chocolatiers?"

"Yes! And what if you created the service design experience of major chocolate factories?"

"I like that," she said, scribbling notes. "Yes, and what if I designed the labels and websites for chocolatiers and their distributors?"

"Yup!"

"What if I was an in-house designer for a chocolate company, and I designed their physical and digital experiences, but also service design, for them?"

"Yes! And you could also have the chocolate company be a design client if you were your own consultant. Let's flip it: How might you bring chocolate into the design world?"

"Mmm," she said. "Hadn't thought of that. Well, I could hold chocolate tastings for designers. Or I could curate and provide chocolate desserts at design conferences. Who doesn't like chocolate?"

And on and on we went. Get it? We were not in boxes, thinking she has to do either chocolate or design, or getting stuck in one rut, overly precious about it. We were blending, flipping, tweaking, and imagining several potential ideas.

 BLEND TWO OR MORE INGREDIENTS OF MEANING

Take two of your ingredients of meaning that stand out to you, and brainstorm creative ways to intersect them. Ask yourself, "How might I apply X to Y?" For example, "How might I apply medicine to writing?" And brainstorm, starting with "What if . . . ?," such as "What if I write a *Grey's Anatomy*-esque screenplay?" Brainstorm for a solid five minutes—remember, you want to dig deep and stretch, so keep going until the timer is done. Then you can flip it and ask yourself, "How might I apply Y to X?" For example, "How might I apply writing to medicine?"

Hopefully, having gone through these brainstorming exercises, you can now see how you can integrate your passions to find *a* pathway to try out, instead of feeling you must choose *one* pathway for the rest of your life (way too much pressure). Also, if you're feeling overwhelmed after brainstorming, don't lose heart.

It's totally normal. Our inner critics love to chime in to tell us that our ideas are ridiculous or we don't have enough resources to bring them to life. Brainstorming is an intentionally generative activity that requires us to suspend our disbelief. You don't have to take one or any of these pathways, but at least see that the range of possibilities for your life is much bigger than what you originally imagined. Remember, keep an open mind. Also remember that new pathways aren't always about making a big, dramatic change; rather, they are about *simply weaving the threads together*.

Blending our ingredients of meaning is also a powerful way to get over that pesky mind-set of not being expert or experienced enough. My client Jade (who you'll get to know more in the Myth of Perfection chapter) did not feel ready or experienced enough to speak on a panel about women in product design because she came from a slightly different industry—art direction for publishing. In fact, she was hired *because of this experience*. Instead of seeing herself as tech-deficient, she had an opportunity to apply her background in art direction to branding in tech. Jade is *cool*—she's the kind of woman who is featured in magazines for her "street style," and she's trying to become more techie? Hell, no. The tech world needs some Jade. Her style, her sensibility, and her understanding of trends and what creates sticky brands are what this tech app needs more than anything in the world, and yet she didn't feel ready to speak because she didn't fit the mold? When we weave our threads together, we focus on what we can give right now.

A LOT OF PEOPLE DON'T KNOW THIS: I PROPOSED TO MY HUSBAND. I didn't have a ring, but I had bought a handmade artisanal bracelet, which came in a tin box that said "Unite" on it, and I put that baby right around his wrist. Of course, there had been an unspoken rule in my family that the man proposes to the woman (same-sex marriage isn't even on the table as an option) with a ring—but I always had an inkling that it was mine to do. And why not? I wanted to marry him and felt it was the time, so I seized my desire as men had done centuries before me. He was surprised and over-joyed. Together, for a moment in time, we flipped a serious script and broke the Myth of Rules. A few family members were not happy to hear the news of how this all went down, so of course I didn't hear the end of it for some time. Backlash is inevitable when we break rules. But it has felt like a worthy price to pay for our unforgettable moment together.

As women, we need to question *all* the invisible rules imposed on us, redefine success for ourselves, and broaden our field of vision to include new possibilities for our lives. It takes courage, but you've got this. You didn't come here to be small. Own your life and design it the way you want. Get in touch with your gifts and share them, whether or not they align neatly with your career. We need you. When more of us break the Myth of Rules, we bring more female perspectives into the world and disrupt old, horribly designed industries, the status quo, and what's been traditionally done for thousands of years (yawn). Together we can create new norms that help shape a better future for us all.

Your New Toolbox

Listed here are all the tools we've explored in this chapter, along with their page numbers so you can quickly reference and practice them whenever you need to.

- Become more aware of your conditioning: use the **Invisible Rules Checklists** (pages 54, 55, 57 and 59).

- Shift rigid mind-sets about your life: move through the **Four Pathway Reframes** (starting on page 61).

- Understand what truly matters: reflect on the **Ingredients of Meaning Process** (starting on page 68).

- Cozy up to death: practice the **Death Meditation** (page 75).

- Generate fresh pathways, ideas, and goals around meaning: work through the **Brainstorming and Blending Process** (starting on page 76).

For further resources, including self-care rituals and meditations for the Myth of Rules, see the appendix.

5

The Myth of Perfection

The Myth of Perfection

SOUNDS LIKE

"I must perform at a high level in all areas of my life without breaking a sweat."

LOOKS LIKE

The tendency to demand perfection in ourselves and others instead of embracing mistakes and the reality of how things are.

MAIN STRATEGY FOR APPROVAL

Being the best at everything and better than others.

POWERS YOU GIVE UP

Your creative confidence, vulnerability, and authenticity.

THE SEXY ARGENTINE TEEN INCHED HIMSELF CLOSER TO the fence around the tennis court. *"¿Permiso, qué hora es?* (Excuse me, what time is it?)," he asked, his dark brown eyes peering through the wire diamonds. I looked down at my tiny plastic watch and froze. I couldn't remember how to tell the time in Spanish. I paused for what seemed an eternity and then managed to spit out a mumble-jumble of words. The young man slowly backed away from the fence, confused. *"Gracias,"* he said. Back at our hotel room in a popular beach town a few hours South of Buenos Aires, my parents poked a little lighthearted fun at me—*"Son las diez menos cuarto* (It's a quarter to ten)," they said, shaking their heads. Even though it was such a tiny incident and they probably don't remember it today, I felt so much embarrassment that I did that thing you see in the movies when the heroine goes to the bathroom to cry and takes a hard look at herself in the mirror, mascara dripping down her face (I know, *dramatic*). At the time, I just knew what I felt in my system: shame and sadness.

It was because of the Myth of Perfection—the reason why I lost most of the fluency of my mother tongue. When I was five years old, my mom would sit at the edge of my bed at night and hold up a mason jar. "For every time you speak a Spanish word, I'll put a penny in the jar," she said. But I shook my head in mortification. "No!" I decided I was no longer going to speak Spanish. It was too difficult, and I wasn't good at it anymore. I had a funny accent and felt embarrassed by my parents' accents when they spoke English. Plus, I was so good at everything else. In my childhood logic, I couldn't afford to suck at anything, as that would ruin my awesome streak of perfection! So, because I was afraid of saying it wrong, and obsessed with getting it right, I lost my mother tongue.

In trying to be the perfect girl who wasn't bad at anything, I lost a connection to my roots. I lost my sense of belonging. This language loss felt like the first time a real rift began to develop between my parents and me and between my home culture and my new culture. My brother and I would be the first generation in many generations not to speak our language fluently. Language signals that we belong—we belong to our families, our cultures, and our tribes. If I could go back in time, I would tell my five-year-old self to stick it out during the awkward period of fumbling through and making mistakes, that it would be worthwhile in the end. I would tell my teenage self, deflated by her blunder, that it still isn't too late to learn. That culture, connections, and roots matter, more than getting an A+ on that paper. But that is what the Myth of Perfection does—it alienates us from others and ourselves.

In my practice and even in my personal life, I see the Myth of Perfection grip far too many women. When we're obsessed with avoiding mistakes, we miss out on the most important learning and growth of our lives. After millennia under the patriarchy, it's the myth with the deepest, gnarliest, thirstiest roots. Think about it. If you want to control people, make them walk on a tightrope, flatten them into a product, shrink them into a box, lather masks onto their faces, and tell them they can't move. Make them feel they aren't worthy as they are. The Myth of Perfection prevents us from taking action on our ideas, lowers our creative confidence, *and* makes us feel as if we're not enough, which in turn drives us to compensate by striving and proving, often in a completely misaligned direction and to the point of utter exhaustion. The opposite of perfection is vulnerability and intimacy—when we allow ourselves to be seen as we are. The only way to deal with the Myth of Perfection is by embracing mistakes while also standing by our own side *unconditionally*, regardless of performance or production. Overcoming the Myth of Perfection is about rehumanizing ourselves as women and retrieving our innermost authenticity. Could there be more important work for us to do?

Fixed Versus Growth Mind-Set

"I could have been in the San Francisco symphony, but instead I'm uploading videos to YouTube," my client Lyndall said, perching her chin on her fist and letting out a big, heavy sigh. A friend had suggested she enter an online music contest because he was sure she could win a cruise to Cozumel, Mexico. For as long as this friend could remember, since the days of growing up in Petaluma, California, Lyndall had been *the* musically gifted one among their friends. So, to please her friend, Lyndall reluctantly agreed. She propped her phone camera up against a chair in her city apartment and started shooting a video of herself playing the clarinet. Four hours later, she reviewed the footage and tossed the phone aside, utterly defeated. None of her performances were good enough.

Suddenly, she was hit by what seemed like a brilliant idea. She'd bake a cake! Yes, you read that correctly. And no, not because she was hungry. She uploaded a video of herself baking a cake and entered *that* into the contest instead. It was a quasi cooking tutorial on how to bake the perfect chocolate cake. "You know, as a joke," she said. "Uh huh. Funny, right?" I, for one, did not laugh at this revelation, but I blinked a few times, fascinated by my client's creative workaround. Lyndall's friends, on the other hand, *did* laugh, proclaiming she was downright hilarious, and everyone skipped away from the scene unscathed. No Mexico this year, not because Lyndall wasn't super musically gifted but because she didn't bother trying!

That was one self-sabotaging pastriarchy (sorry, I couldn't help myself). And the pastriarchy chef? You guessed it—the Myth of Perfection. For Lyndall, it started when she was a little girl. When she was only four, teachers and parents singled her out as a musical genius and groomed her to one day perform with one of the major symphonies. Except that day never came, even after years of her being lauded as gifted.

In college, Lyndall gave up on her career as a professional musician, and one thing became clear in our coaching together. She, like me, like many of us, didn't like sounding or looking bad. She didn't like fumbling or making mistakes, and she certainly didn't like losing or failing, because that might imply she *wasn't* naturally gifted. Any professional musician will tell you, it's hard to get to the next level if you don't let yourself fail and continuously be a beginner again and again. But being naturally gifted was one thing Lyndall wanted to hold on to and protect with all her mighty heart—the precious notion that she was talented and that she failed because she didn't bother to try, not because she was bad. And who can blame her?

If you were a good girl growing up in the patriarchy, odds are you too were patted on your head for being gifted. And you'd think this is a good thing, but alas, it isn't. In a study that videotaped parents giving their children praise, girls and boys received the same amount of praise, but parents of boys used a greater percentage of process praise, which focuses on effort and strategies, than did parents of girls, who praised them instead for personal traits such as intelligence.[1] Researchers found that children who received process praise had a more positive attitude toward challenges five years later. Why? Because they had developed what Stanford University professor Carol Dweck calls a growth, versus fixed, mind-set.[2]

A growth mind-set is when you believe that abilities can change, while a fixed mind-set is when you believe abilities, such as intelligence, are unchangeable, as in you can't get better at them through practice—you either have them or you don't.

Of course, having a growth mind-set is so much better because you're more likely to take on challenges and less likely to quit, leading to more positive growth. Susan Levine, a psychology professor at the University of Chicago, shared from her research: "Later, boys were more likely to have positive attitudes about academic challenges than girls and to believe that intelligence could be improved."[3] Dweck has long shown that bright girls—those with high IQ and straight A's—are more likely to throw in the towel when faced with confusing, hard material they can't ace right away.[4]

Just as we saw happen with Lyndall, if your parents and teachers told you over and over again that you were born with some special gift or trait, you'll be less likely to take on challenges that risk fail-ure and that might suggest you actually *don't* have that trait, since you've become so invested in maintaining that standard, reputa-tion, or badge of honor. Basically, you'll quit far too early or not even bother playing. I have a vivid memory from a childhood visit back to Argentina, sitting at my grandmother's kitchen table and drawing a mermaid. It was one of the first drawings I recall mak-ing. My grandma, Goddess bless her heart, an artist herself, loved my mermaid so much that she told all my cousins I was an *excep-tional* artist (I mean, I *did* put eyelashes on that mermaid), and she pinned it to the fridge for all to behold. My grandma was giving me what seemed to be harmless encouragement. And it worked; my brain was lit on fire by surges of dopamine. Back home in Can-ada, I drew some more and waited for the world to praise me the way my grandmother had back in Argentina, but there were only crickets. Chirp. Chirp. *Look teachers, look!* "Yes, that's nice, they would say, but maybe try adding this . . ."

Whaaaaa? I thought. *You mean, I'm not an epic mermaid-artist?!* It turned out I might have been an average drawer (and obviously a beginner) after all. Even though I enjoyed it, I didn't draw for years after that.

The opposite of process praise is person praise ("You're an amazing singer!" "You're super smart!" "You're *so* nice!"), which my grandma didn't know she was giving when she told me I was exceptionally artistic. Is person praise actually damaging, though? Well (*putting hands together awkwardly*), looks like it. This kind of praise seems particularly hurtful to girls, as one study showed that person praise deflated the motivation of upper-elementary girls but not boys.[5] According to old-school motivation researchers Edward L. Deci and Richard M. Ryan,[6] girls may be more easily hooked on feedback because they pay more attention to whether they've pleased the evaluator, which in turn makes them more sensitive to feeling (and, IMHO, *being*) controlled by feedback. Could it be true?

In another study,[7] elementary school children were given informational, controlling, or mixed (a clever concoction of informational and controlling) feedback for their performance on a puzzle task. An example of controlling praise is telling a child that if she performs well, she'll get a chance to perform again or that the researchers will have useable data for their study. Performance becomes attached to a desired outcome and there's a pressure to perform well. Informational praise is simply stating a positive observation of how someone is performing, such as "you're doing really well." Controlling praise hurts the motivation of all the kiddos (duh), but mixed praise puts a dent in girls' interest while actually emboldening boys' interest. The researchers concluded that, yes, girls picked up on the controlling aspects of mixed praise, whereas boys focused on the informational aspects, so they were more than fine.

Our fear of criticism and failure holds us back from kicking ass because we don't give ourselves the chance to shine. One study in particular really bothered me: women didn't perform as well as men on a spatial task if they were given the option to skip the question, but if they had to answer every question, they performed just as well as men.[8] Imagine all the hundreds of thousands, if not millions, of women who miss opportunities because they don't bother playing! It's always best to toss your hat into the ring and say What-the-heck-why-not-let-me-try-it-and-see.

Again, all of this starts when we're really young and gets internalized into our psyches. How did your parents respond to you when you made a mistake or when you failed? Dweck and her colleague Kyla Haimovitz showed that parents who see failure as bad get fixated on their children's performance rather than their learning, which leads their children to develop fixed mind-sets. Their work highlighted that children do inherit their parents' beliefs and behaviors in response to failure.

It's no wonder so many of my clients describe feeling that they're "not ready yet," and their work "isn't good enough" to begin or show, well into their twenties and thirties. Or, even worse, they think things about themselves in fixed terms, like "I'm just not a writer," and quit while they're ahead. That's when I (metaphorically) shake them by the shoulders and call them out on this myth—heroine, you're walking around like a zombie hypnotized by the Myth of Perfection. Let's build up your creative confidence.

Creative Confidence

According to design thinkers Tom Kelley and David M. Kelley, "the combination of thought and action defines creative confidence: the ability to come up with new ideas and the courage to try them out."[9] That last part is key. We women have no shortage of ideas and gifts, but how many of us follow through and take action?

Under the Myth of Perfection, we're gripped by a great deal of fear, which inevitably causes us to procrastinate, overanalyze, avoid, delay, and do everything in our power *not* to do the thing. Perfectionism blocks action, and ultimately growth, by keeping us safe within our comfort zone.

Jade knows. After ten years as an art director in publishing in New York City, she moved to Seattle to apply her brand expertise to the tech industry. "My boss handed his team over to me to lead, which is both thrilling and terrifying," she said. Jade was feeling serious waves of nausea during work, sneaking to the bathroom between meetings to lock herself in a stall and throw up or hyperventilate. Responsible for the creative direction and redesign of a popular app with millions of users, she was playing outside her comfort zone. What if she got it wrong? What if she got it right? What if she fucked this up? What if she rocked it? This was the first time Jade had felt like a beginner since childhood, and she was feeling like a total imposter.

"There is plenty of tech-lingo I'm unfamiliar with, which makes me feel like I have no idea what I'm talking about or even doing here," she told me before starting our coaching. As a new member of the executive team, she was constantly terrified of "saying the wrong thing," so she held back her opinions.

"What does being taken seriously mean to you?" I asked.

"It means others view me as an executive. A leader who is eloquent and knows what she's saying. A leader who is in control," she said.

"You don't feel like you're there yet," I reflected back to her.

"Right. I don't want to say the wrong thing. I certainly don't want to embarrass my boss or the company."

"How do you think you'll get to a place where you'll be taken seriously?"

"When I know all the tech-lingo. I'm just not a techie."

Aha! Herein lies the catch-22 of the Myth of Perfection: it prevents us from taking the very action (i.e., practice) we need to take in order to get where we want to go, keeping us stuck in a self-defeating loop. How would Jade learn to speak if she never spoke? In fact, she turned down the opportunity to speak on that panel about women in product design because she "didn't feel ready," even though she was literally the vice president of product design and the only female executive at her company. "I want to make sure I put my absolute best foot forward," she told me, adjusting her heavy-rimmed glasses. "So, I turned it down."

You heard me the first time: the way to break this myth is to *do the thing you're scared to do.* The way for Jade to get better at speaking is by speaking. I know, I know—so many self-help gurus tell us, "Do the thing you're scared to do." Ummm . . . thanks. "Have confidence in yourself!" Ummm . . . thanks. So what's missing? *How* do you do the thing you're scared to do? Design thinking can help: we build creative confidence by getting out of our heads when we *make something* and *engage someone* (sounds simple, but there's more to it, so read on).

Prototyping

It's time to turn to our third design mind-set and *make something.* When I learned how to prototype at the d.school, a whole new world of possibility opened up to me. A prototype is a small, quick, easy-to-make, easy-to-break version of your idea or goal. Prototypes allow you to test your ideas without too much skin in the game. (If only we viewed all our ideas through the lens of prototyping, we would save ourselves so much time, money, and heartache.) Because prototypes are *purposefully* imperfect, they are only *approximations* of your ideas and are meant to be eventually thrown out. That's the beauty! Here are some characteristics of prototypes:

- Cheap

- Scrappy

- Constrained

- "Low-fidelity"

- Approximation of the idea

- Quick and easy to make

- Quick and easy to test

If you're not used to putting yourself out there, prototyping is a great way to build creative confidence and take mini uncomfortable leaps that won't terrify and paralyze you. It's okay if you don't know *exactly* where you're going or what you're doing. The point of a prototype is to help you discover that by giving you more information. It's a way to engage with the world, get quick feedback, and course-correct—the foundation of all learning!

Why Prototype?

Prototyping is *the* antidote for perfectionism, and when done with awareness, it can help you learn, stretch, and grow in ways you never imagined. Prototypes help us do the following:

- Break perfectionistic all-or-nothing thinking ("either I do my idea perfectly as it is in my mind or not at all") by shrinking ideas down to a middle ground.

- Break our obsession with looking put together, because we must embrace the prototype's purposeful scrappiness (and, yes, ugliness).

97

- Have a deliberate and safe space to make mistakes (no high stakes!), supercharging our learning (yay!).

- Reduce our high standards into sober, realistic ones that help us gauge the true feasibility of our ideas.

- Learn more about what we *actually* like and don't like instead of what we *think* we like and don't like.

- Test our assumptions and course-correct without too many resources and without quitting our day jobs.

- Make better decisions about which direction to take and which idea to run with, because we have more data about what works and doesn't work.

About those last two points: prototyping allows us to "fail early and fast." It helps us in the process of elimination. I've also worked with a lot of women who, for example, want to bridge into freelancing or becoming their own boss. You can prototype that pathway by taking on *one* client while working full-time. Too many of us think this is a conflict of interest because we're caught by the Myth of Rules. Unless it's written in ink in a contract, you're safe to test this pathway. Even one client can give you a taste of what's possible. What did you learn in acquiring that client? Did you like it? Would you do it again? Were you helpful to them? How much did they pay? How much would they be willing to pay? All these questions can get you answers through prototyping.

After graduating from college, I strongly considered offering brand and web design for other coaches. Before I announced it to the world, and updated my services and website, I ran a prototype by taking on one design client in addition to all my coaching clients, and guess what? I discovered it wasn't for me. I crossed it off my list.

It turns out I like full permission to be free and independent when it comes to my creativity, and design was not the way I was going to make money. Test and eliminate. The process of elimination is how we course-correct. We don't necessarily stumble on the right, perfect pathway for us; we go through several prototypes (ideally over a few weeks and not decades) before we realize which one we're truly able to commit to and manifest right now. It's a whole different way of operating in the world, but embrace it and it will change your life.

Getting Started

Before you can make something, you have to decide what you're making. Sometimes you instantly know, though I recommend doing a creative brainstorm (refer back to the section on brainstorming in the Myth of Rules) to generate a handful of options before choosing an idea to prototype. For example, Jade and I both took out sticky notes and set a timer for five minutes. We wanted to stretch ourselves to get at least ten ideas, and our guiding question was "How might Jade speak more?" Here were some of the ideas we came up with. She could . . .

- Park herself on the corner of a subway station and speak her mind.

- Gather some friends on a Friday night and present about her work project over a glass of wine.

- Start a podcast about women in product design.

- Do a brown-bag lunch and invite a few colleagues to hear her thoughts on their latest project.

- Lead a yoga class after work at a friend's co-working space.

Once you have a handful of ideas, prioritize them and choose your favorite one. Follow your joy and curiosity. Which idea gives you tingles? Pick one that stretches you a little bit. Don't spend too much time on this step because you can choose another idea later, which brings me again to my favorite mantra about prototyping: *Don't be precious.* Choose one. If it doesn't give you joy, scrap it and try another. You've got this.

How to Make Your Prototype

Break Your Ideas Way Down

"If I'm being honest with myself," started Jade, "I'd love to start a podcast about women in product design. I feel like that would help me share my voice and expertise."

Ideas are wonderful because they come out as uninhibited babies or as colorful, bold drag queens in all shapes and sizes, unapologetically themselves. But at this stage, our ideas need serious downsizing. As someone who has started a podcast, I knew that this process has multiple steps and substeps. Imagine if, as we left the session, I said, "Okay! By the next time I see you, you will have started a podcast about women in product design!" High five!

Knowing my sweet Jade, she would never have started the podcast—not because she couldn't but because that next step would be far too big and overwhelming, exciting as it may be. That's *why* we prototype. Prototypes must be *really* small and easy to do. Let's start at the easiest and smallest step, and then we can build up.

"Jade, what would you need to record an episode?"

"I would need to do some research, buy a mic, and write out a script—"

"Too big and too much work. Is buying a mic the only way you can record?"

"I mean, I could record on my phone, I guess."

"Perfect. How about recording a voice memo on your phone and keeping it to three minutes?"

When we shrink an idea way down, we *set ourselves up for success* (another one of our design thinking–inspired mind-sets) by removing barriers to action, making ourselves a thousand times more likely to get it done. Here I removed the barrier of equipment, and the whole script/time thing, because with three minutes, she could improvise or write a relatively short script instead of a feature-length screenplay.

Notice that this isn't necessarily about breaking the "start a podcast" step into smaller steps—that's an oversimplified view. If I had broken it down into smaller steps, her first step would have been to buy some equipment, which would have led her down a rabbit hole. What we've found here is a *prototype*—a smaller version of a full-blown, fancy, professionally recorded episode—which she can get quick feedback on later.

Embrace Constraints

Prototypes help us break the Myth of Perfection by asking us to embrace constraints. Designers love constraints! Mindful constraints engender creativity while breaking perfectionism. We don't have time for overthinking about our precious creations when we have only two minutes to make the darn thing. We simply have to move on. Also, putting in fewer resources will make you less precious. Here are the top constraints that will help you design your prototype.

TIME AND QUANTITY

There's a story about a woodworking professor who challenged her two classes to make a beautiful yet functional table. She told Class A that they could make only one table, but they had the entire semester to work on it. She told Class B that they had to make as many tables as possible together and then choose the best one at the end. Which class do you think made the best-designed table? Class B. When it comes to prototyping, less time per prototype and a larger number of prototypes is better. Why? Because we get better and learn through *iteration*, not by getting tense and precious and laboring over *one* thing as if our lives depend on it.

So, what could you create in under an hour? What about under ten minutes? Instead of spending an hour on one prototype, what if you spent ten minutes and made six in an hour? Increasing the number of prototypes will help you be less precious. In Jade's case, I challenged her to make at least five three-minute voice memos (and constrained her making time to one hour total). Going for quantity will help you let go of the need for them to be perfect. But sink in a limited amount of time, and practice timing yourself.

SIZE

If I haven't hammered this home yet, I will again: ideas are big, but prototypes are small. One day, Jade will create hour-long podcast episodes, but her prototype will be only three minutes long, like a teaser or a sampler. Here are some examples of shrinking an idea in terms of size.

- An art exhibition becomes *one* painting (which could be reduced even further through scrappier materials and equipment).

- A freelance business becomes *one* client (which could be reduced even further by downsizing the deliverable—for example, putting together *three* slides or making *one* logo sketch).

- A ten-day silent meditation retreat becomes *one* five-minute meditation at home.

- A new career in management becomes *one* conversation with a manager or *one* person to manage.

MATERIALS AND COST

In Jade's case, we went from a podcast studio setup to voice memos on her phone. Many user experience designers use pencil and paper to imagine possible user flows for a new app. You can reduce materials for virtually any idea, and there are more tools than ever to enable our creativity, so no excuses! Let's say one of my lifelong dreams is to make a feature-length film about my trip to Thailand. What are some other media formats, besides film, I could use to capture the essence of my trip? I could print out photographs of key moments from my trip and arrange them in a particular order, making a kind of comic strip. This would help me capture the concept and get feedback quickly. If I wanted to bring it closer to the medium of film, I could still stay scrappy by filming groups of friends reenacting a moment in Thailand using my cell phone's camera. In other words, don't go fancy; go *scrappy*. Keep materials cheap, or brainstorm alternatives. Think outside the box. Reducing materials will help keep the cost of your prototype low, which ideally would be zero, because the more money you sink into it, the more attached you'll become. Architects and industrial designers make models all the time, so this isn't anything new, but my point is that you can do it for *any* idea or goal of yours, and that's pretty revolutionary. Here are examples of ways to reduce cost by reducing materials.

- Instead of buying a 3-D printer, use modeling clay.
- Instead of hiring a developer to build you a new website, use an online web development tool like Squarespace or even simple notecards to imagine what it'll look like.
- Instead of renting a ballroom, use your friend's garage.

 IDENTIFY YOUR PROTOTYPES

Focus on a big and scary dream of yours (you know, the one you've been delaying) and come up with five ways to prototype it by embracing one of these resource con-straints. Remember, make your prototypes ridiculously small and easy to do. When you think you've gotten small, look again, and urge yourself to break it down even more. I could . . .

_____

_____

_____

Put Yourself Out There

Making a prototype is one thing; sharing it is another. Sharing makes us vulnerable because we open ourselves up to judgment and criticism. We allow ourselves to be seen as we are, in process, figuring it out, and messy. We also admit that we're exploring, testing a pathway, trying to do something outside of the box, which feels uncomfortable because most of the world is pretty square. We risk breaking people's ideas and labels of us as "the teacher" or "the analytical one," and that can feel odd (remember, most people resist change). There's a ton of reasons why *not* sharing is easier. But that is not how we grow. We can learn to thicken our skin a bit by playing with what I like to call our *vulnerability edge*.

Your vulnerability edge is that uncomfortable sweet spot between comfort and growth. It's that place of risk where we're vulnerable to failure and judgment.

Let's say I draw a circle and put you in it. We'll label this circle *comfort*. Everything outside that circle is discomfort. The line of the circle—and the liminal space around it—is your vulnerability edge.

Growth happens when we let ourselves touch this edge. Play with this edge. Stand in this edge. Sit with this edge. The more we touch it, the more the line moves back and the circle expands—the more we grow into who we want to become. For all you yoginis,

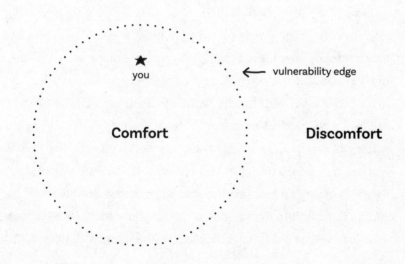

you know what I'm talking about. It's that place when you're in pigeon pose and it stings in your hip, but if you stay with the sting a bit longer by taking deep breaths, you'll notice your body start to melt, stretch, and enter a new level of flexibility and good feelings you didn't know were possible. That is, until you hit your next edge. The edge never goes away; it only gets pushed back. Growth happens *only* when we can be with the discomfort of our edge.

Let's circle back to Jade.

"All right, Jade," I said. "Who will you share your voice memo with?"

"No one," she said with dread, covering her face.

"Don't worry," I assured her. "Let's find your vulnerability edge."

Remember, the edge is where all growth happens. Many coaches and self-help people are all about leaping over the edge into completely new territory. The problem with leaps is that they can give us too many failures early on, and if we're under the spell of this myth, we'll get too discouraged to keep going. We want to find that sweet spot, right at your edge—that place that feels scary enough (because without fear, there ain't no growth) but not paralyzing.

Let's plot some possible sharing actions for Jade on a sharing spectrum. A *sharing action* is exactly what it sounds like—a behavior (ideally small, even though it can feel emotionally big) that involves you sharing yourself and being vulnerable. Each sharing action has a level of intensity, which feels different for each person. Some people feel more comfortable reciting their new poem in front of strangers at a café than at a holiday party their close relatives will be attending. You can modulate the intensity of sharing by changing up and playing around with various elements, including the medium or channel by which you share (in a Facebook news feed versus on a conference stage), the number of people and the quality of those relationships (one or two close friends versus a sea of strangers), and the context (a Friday night potluck in your home versus a facilitated creativity workshop you paid for).

Now, for our sharing spectrum, let us lay out these sharing actions so that we can eventually identify our vulnerability edge. On one side of the sharing spectrum, we have sheer comfort—you know, the kind you experience when you're napping in a pile of really soft bunnies—and on the other side of the spectrum, we have terror—you know, the kind you experience when, in a dream, you realize you're naked in public and everyone is pointing and laughing. Most of us would prefer to nap with bunnies, of course, but that isn't where growth happens, is it? Growth happens as we inch toward terror without actually touching it. With Jade, we brainstormed the spectrum of ways she could share her voice memo, going from comfortable to increasingly scary.

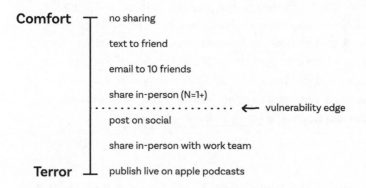

Comfort — no sharing

text to friend

email to 10 friends

share in-person (N=1+)

← vulnerability edge

post on social

share in-person with work team

Terror — publish live on apple podcasts

"Okay, Jade, looking at this list, where's your vulnerability edge? Be honest." She paused. "Texting the voice memo to a friend feels vulnerable, but I'd probably get over it. I feel like sharing it in person and both of us listening to it, that feels more uncomfortable to me. Sharing with a group of friends while they all listen feels like death." We found her edge: share the voice memo with a friend in person. Scary enough while not paralyzing. Being with the discomfort of the vulnerability edge is the very heart of creative confidence and allows you to develop the courage to manifest and show your brilliance to the world.

 ### FIND YOUR VULNERABILITY EDGE

Think about a gift, talent, idea, or project you're afraid to share with others. You can also think back to one of your prototypes from the previous exercise. List the sharing actions involved in that project or prototype with various degrees of intensity and scariness, and then plot them on the sharing spectrum shown here. Be honest with yourself and circle your vulnerability edge. Remember, if you're too conservative, you won't learn. But if you're too bold, you may inadvertently burn yourself by going too hard too soon (also a great way to self-sabotage). Use your wisdom to find that edge that hits that sweet spot. Once you've identified the sharing action at your vulnerability's edge, go put it into action. You know, out there, in the real world. It's how you'll learn.

As you can see, prototyping is an effective way to start deflating the Myth of Perfection and moving toward your goals. It won't always be comfortable, and it may be scary at times, but I promise that if you take these small steps, testing things out, being okay with trying a variety of new things, it will help build that creative confidence that leads you on the path that *you* design.

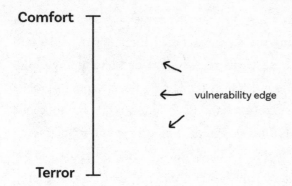

The Good Girl Achiever

We've seen how the Myth of Perfection can cripple your creative confidence and block your ability to bring forth your ideas and gifts into the world, but there's another, equally dangerous way it hooks into us: it tells us that we're not enough. One of the most common "not enoughs" I've witnessed among good girls, especially those who grew up being told they were gifted, is that they feel they're not achieving enough. Many of them describe not doing enough, not being far ahead enough, or not going fast enough.

In a capitalist culture, success is about climbing the ladder or striving to the top of the mountain and staking your flag. It's about going higher and being greater. Our entire culture is about who can do it best and who can be the winner. Daughters of immigrants like me will tell ya—we were raised to work and study like the Energizer Bunny. Since I was a little girl, my psyche has been engulfed by a primary family narrative with my father busting his ass, which allowed him to leave his country and pursue (as well as give his children) unbounded economic opportunities in the land of the free. But at what cost? By the time I was sixteen, I had been to at least ten different schools. My father's career opportunities kept growing and opening up, so we pursued them, again and again and again. By the time I was in college, I had barely any childhood friends left. We lost touch, made new friends, only to move on from them a year or two later. Even today, while my mother's siblings and their families stay huddled together in her hometown in Argentina (literally living a block away from each other, à la *My Big Fat Greek Wedding*), my brother, parents, and I are scattered all over the United States because we've prioritized our careers, upward mobility, and autonomy. Capitalism creates more *individualist* societies. This land was literally built by immigrants seeking freedom, so our puritan work ethic and obsession with stories of perseverance and grit are so deeply ingrained that deprogramming them can feel like a very steep hill.

According to a recent study, nearly half of Americans reported feeling alone or left out, with one in four saying they rarely or never feel that there are people who truly understand them.[10] The National Institute of Mental Health reports that at least 17.3 million adults have experienced major depression and almost one-third of Americans will experience some kind of anxiety disorder (e.g., social anxiety, phobia, post-traumatic stress disorder) in their lifetime.[11] Obviously, these stats are connected to our overall health, as between 1996 and 2003, we spent over $180 billion on chronic diseases like heart disease and diabetes and have a serious obesity problem.[12] We consume far more than any other large country in the world,[13] extracting the Earth's natural resources to produce goods, which we use only briefly before tossing them back into the environment as hundreds of billions of tons of trash. The way we're living isn't working. And capitalism has a role to play. Capitalism is about nonstop *production*. We work and overwork to earn

110

so that we can consume more and more and fill a deeper void of chronic dissatisfaction. We live in a society virtually obsessed with *doing* over being. We're seen as valuable if and only if we produce things, ideas, and products that have value in a market. We are expected to be linear, industrious, and efficient people instead of full, complex, multifaceted humans, which is why women gripped by this myth often find it hard to take breaks and rest because they're hooked on producing work.

In hopes of equalizing with men in the workplace, a lot of recent feminism of the 2000s has aligned itself with capitalist ideas. Most pervasive is the idea that women can become the ultimate "work woman" (like men), an ideal that only bolsters an old paradigm. By this, I mean a woman who earns and works as much as, if not more than, men, dresses in corporate attire; and aims to climb the corporate ladder in order to gain more status, influence, and wealth. Some people call this *corporate* feminism—and it puts us in the same trap as it puts men, as a woman derives her value from whether or not she creates wealth and value (to the same degree that men do, if not more). I think this is why so many of us women have issues with motherhood. We see motherhood as a threat to getting ahead in our careers. And our attempt to remedy the situation has been to create a more equitable workplace (I'm all for it), but there's an underlying issue that isn't being addressed: we're still caught in a game of making money, upward ascension, abiding to the system, and aligning our value in a way that capitalism defines it. But is that where you want your value to be?

Everything about human beings is extraordinary regardless of outward, visible production; we have these hearts and lungs and cells that are miraculous, working their invisible magic every day. Even the most "unproductive" person is still massively productive in her body—digestive juices breaking down her food and billions of neurons firing in her mind. Women are also extraordinary, regardless of production, having cycles and giving life or upholding and performing self-defined femininity. By virtue of living, breathing, and existing, we are worthy.

Embracing Being

As good girls under the spell of this myth, we need to unhook our worthiness from work—*doing*—and hook it back to something far more human and fundamental—*being*. How? Let me suggest two ways. The first way is by practicing the following mantra, over and over again. Reprogramming happens through repetition.

 PRACTICE THIS MANTRA: "I AM WORTHY SIMPLY BECAUSE I EXIST."

Mantras work best when written out and placed somewhere. Where could you place this mantra in your life? Think bathroom mirror, car dashboard, or your daily planner.

Clients tell me that when they repeat this mantra to themselves throughout the day, they feel their shoulder blades melt down their back and they let a sigh of relief escape their mouths. They can feel that no matter what they did or didn't do, no matter how many items linger on their to-do list, it's not a reflection of their value and worthiness deep down. It allows them to reclaim something deep within. The myth loosens its grip, and they feel more at home within themselves.

The second way is to start a meditation practice. You've probably heard people say this to you many times before, but meditation
is essentially the art of nondoing (which is why it makes so many
of us "doers" uncomfortable). Going back to the idea of prototypes,
we can start really small with meditation. Practice it for five or
ten minutes, simply focusing on your breath with a soft, gentle,
and kind attention. Expect thoughts. That's normal! There is no
failing at meditation, I promise. You can have millions of thoughts
and still be meditating. You can come in and out of presence and
daydreaming several times and still be meditating. Meditation is
not about clearing your mind; it is about learning to be with *what is*
without trying to *do* anything about it, okay? Practicing nondoing
and embracing being through meditation will show you benefits if
you keep at it. As one meditation teacher once told me, "We brush
our teeth, but what about our minds?"

By practicing the mantra and meditation, you'll begin unhook-
ing your worth from work and move from doing to being. The
price you'll pay otherwise is too high. If your worthiness hinges

PRACTICE A
NONDOING MEDITATION

Grab your phone and set your timer for ten minutes. I like
to use the Insight Timer app, which allows me to set bells.
Close your eyes and focus on your breath for ten minutes. If
your mind wanders, come back to your breath. It's truly that
simple. (In the Myth of Sacrifice, we'll also talk about where
you can insert a meditation practice throughout your day,
so hang tight.) You might decide to pause now and try it out
for two minutes as a little sample warm-up and then come
back to me.

113

on performance, you'll basically do anything to be a top performer. *Anything.*

In 1996, Kerri Strug won the gymnastics gold medal for the American team *even though she had a broken ankle.* This became a huge media sensation, an unforgettable story about a girl who "persisted" to become a champion and global phenomenon. But ya gotta admit, it's a bit twisted. Right around that time, I was also in competitive ice skating and decided that I too would push through my fever (even though my mother insisted I stay home) and win first place in my little local competition. I was so proud. My parents were proud, and since then, many have called me determined, a wonderful compliment I could add to my collection. My ice-skating incident—inspired by Kerri—was a lesson in persistence, wasn't it? Ignore the needs of our bodies and push through to get to the top. This conditioning is at the root of my good girl coping strategy. No breaks. Never mind pain. Push. Push. Push. Well, you know how that ends.

Burnout and Exhaustion

The expectation of doing more—coupled with rule following (Myth of Rules) and not using our voices to assert our needs (Myth of Harmony)—is a recipe for burnout. Under the Myth of Perfection, we work our asses off to keep up with impossible standards, to have it all, while dabbing little pearls of sweat from our foreheads. Maybe you've heard of "paddling duck syndrome," when you look like you are gliding effortlessly on the serene lake, but under the water's surface your little duck legs are scrambling like a motor. That duck face, though. Super sweet, super relaxed.

In the first half of the twentieth century, before the women's rights movement of the 1960s, most American women had defined, limited roles (e.g., wife, mother). While second-wave feminism gave us the choice to have as many roles as we'd like, the Myth of Perfection tricks us into performing all of them simultaneously with "effortless perfection." If you've watched *The Incredibles*, you know the trope—Mrs. Incredible is Elastigirl, designed to be everywhere at once, juggle everyone's demands, and warp her body into a trampoline or a parachute, depending on the rescue need. As a top performer and quite literally a superhero, she manages all of it without breaking a sweat. For ladies like us with human bodies, however, it's impossible to be Elastigirl, and we put way too much pressure on ourselves to perform at her superhuman level.

Under the Myth of Perfection, we have persistent feelings of failure no matter how much we do. Even when a client has accomplished the most incredible feat and come so far in her life (say, raised millions of dollars for her company), she walks into our session talking about what she hasn't done for the day and what she has yet to do. Heroine, the to-do list is a treadmill that never stops. So maybe it's time to trade in the treadmill for something else.

Setting Work Boundaries

One of my clients, Zoe, was drowning in the feeling that she was never doing enough. "I'm working myself to the bone," she told me, tucking her hair behind her ear. As we sat in my office, the fog was rolling in, and Zoe looked teary-eyed and hopeless, wondering why, oh why, she was doing this to herself again. I mean,

115

this poor lady's daily commute was one and a half hours each way through thick San Francisco Bay Area traffic. When she got home, she would lock herself in her apartment with a bottle of wine and zone out for hours binge-watching Netflix and shoveling caramel popcorn into her mouth. She had no social life outside of work and was sweeping her real passions for environmental conservation, human rights, and art under the rug. This wasn't *just* about earning a paycheck and a living, since many of her co-workers seemed to have a life outside of work. It was clear that the Myth of Perfection was working its spell on her.

She was gripped by an addiction to achieve—achieve success, milestones, objectives, results, performance metrics, bonuses, and, last but not least, validation from her co-workers and managers. Every time she achieved something, it filled her bucket of worthiness. And every time she was not being a busy, neurotic bee or overachieving, she wondered if she was good for nuthin'.

Zoe was caught in one of the most common ways this myth catches us—attaching her worth to her work.

Zoe was so hooked, she kept canceling her Tinder and Bumble dates to stay later at work. She developed a black Tinder thumb. Zoe killed romantic prospects because she was married to, committed to, and monogamous with her job.

Another client was so enslaved by her work that I said to her, "Lemme ask you something. If your job was a boyfriend and it treated you this way, what would you do?" Without hesitation, she said, "Break up with his ass!" Then she paused and said, "But it isn't so easy for work!" You know you're gripped by this myth if you put up with major shit from your job.

We all have some degree of this going on, whether we like to admit it or not. Maybe we're not as extreme as Zoe, but if we grew up as good girls under this myth, with a love for achievement, we definitely need to take a hard, sweet, sober look at our work boundaries.

What are the ways we can protect ourselves from overworking?

For Zoe, we listed concrete behaviors she could try as a week-long experiment (because she was very skeptical and afraid to peel back at work) to see what would happen.

1. She would leave work every day at five o'clock.

2. She would not respond to certain emails right away, but only after two days.

3. She would put "busy" blocks in her calendar so that she couldn't attend unnecessary meetings and would instead work on jump-starting an art business. (This one felt most naughty!)

4. She would not work on the weekend for more than two hours.

As her coach, I kept her accountable. I also felt pretty confident this would work with Zoe because she was such a hyperachiever. Sharp as she was, peeling back at work would mean she would still be outperforming 99 percent of her team. Though she knew it would be hard and would feel uncomfortable at first, she was excited about the experiment and curious whether anyone would notice.

But she hesitated for a moment. "I have a performance review around the corner, and I'm hoping to get promoted to manager."

"It's a risk, isn't it? Let's see what you can get away with." We shook on it, and she was off.

So what happened when Zoe set these work boundaries? Well, for one, she felt like a human being again, as if her bones and flesh

117

were filling out. She needed to deal with the guilt and the anxiety that kept creeping up on her—that the world would implode if she weren't there to keep it all together. When Zoe learned to let go and back away from the work, sure, things didn't happen in the most "perfect" way, but she admitted that she gained some space to breathe, and that was worth any perceived blows to quality. Yes, her mental well-being was more important than the quality of the work. Yes, because she was more important than the work. And she was beginning to see that.

Zoe came back to our next session filled with utter disbelief: "Nobody really cares how much you work." Her performance review was stellar, and she got a promotion. In other words, she was fine. More than fine, even with all her work boundaries. Her manager even commented that she seemed more confident and relaxed. She was able to dedicate time to her creative side business and felt less bitter about the time work was taking away from her other passions. Zoe was happier both at work and outside it.

Okay, my sweet overachiever good girls: if you want to work to live instead of live to work, you need some solid work boundaries. Don't expect yourself to have the willpower to disengage

 SET YOUR WORK BOUNDARIES

What are three work boundaries or preventive moves you can make this week so work doesn't take over your life? Borrow some ideas from Zoe and make your own new work rules. Write them down in your journal. Put new engagements and time blocks in your calendar. Chop, chop.

from work, because your good girl programming will surely take the steering wheel. You need to make some practical, preventive moves.

The number one recommendation I make to my clients is to put blocks in the calendar that close out their workday—ideally something prepaid and prescheduled with accountability, like a fitness class with a friend or a dinner date at a highly coveted restaurant. This gives you no choice but to power down. And, for heaven's sake, leave your laptop at work! But don't deplete your reserves with endless happy hours either; work boundaries should help you focus on your creativity, pleasure, and nourishing self-care rituals (something we'll dive into under the Myth of Sacrifice)—activities that fill your cup back up so you can wake up the next day like a fresh newborn babe instead of a dehydrated pineapple.

Clearing Your Plate

Once you've put some work boundaries in place, we can talk about clearing that plate of yours. Under the Myth of Perfection, we internalize the expectation to be "super," ignore the realities of role conflict, and bloat our calendars. Let's actively counteract this tendency by lightening the weight on our shoulders and all the demands of our to-do list.

Keep Your Plate Spacious

A few days before I meet with a new client, I ask her to fill out a survey about how she's been feeling recently. Here's a typical answer: "Good, but overwhelmed with making sure I'm eating the

CLEAR YOUR PLATE

Write a list of your commitments, including things you said yes to but that you aren't excited about or really meant to say no to. These also might be thought of as the logistics and operations of life that claw away at your energy and take up too much time. They can also be things that feel more like "shoulds" or obligations.
Here's an example of a list you might write.

- Host dinner for the family next Saturday.
- Go to Atlanta in July.
- Write out the brief for Hiromi.
- Go grocery shopping.

Create four columns and write the following empowering verbs at the top.

Task	Eliminate	Delegate	Automate	Ask for Help

First, let's define these actions. *Eliminate* is obvious—take it off your list and it ceases to exist. *Delegate* is when you request that somebody else do the task. That's pretty clear. *Asking for help* is different from delegating in that you're still doing the task, but you're doing it with someone or having someone take part of it off your plate. But what about automate? To *automate* is to build a system that makes the behavior easier to do on a repeating basis. For example, to automate grocery shopping, use a tool like Instacart, which lets you set up a repertoire of groceries that you get weekly, or sign up for the subscribe and save option on Amazon. The point is that you're not spending loads of time thinking about it and doing it every week.

Your next step is to slot your different tasks into the columns. Get all those annoying "should" activities off your plate and into one of these buckets. It's amazing what eliminating can do. Oftentimes we think we have to do something, but it turns out we don't always have to; am I right?

right food and enough of it, spending enough time with everyone I care about, learning new skills because I *really* want to get better at coding and do a thousand other things like paint, write a children's book that I can illustrate, sing, et cetera." Not only do we need to wipe things off our plates, we also need to stop piling them on. In our desire to do more and measure up to others, we make food towers on our plates like we're at a free buffet. You know that saying "Your eyes are bigger than your stomach"? Well, sometimes your eyes are bigger than the twenty-four-hour day.

In the same way, when you're trying to do everything at once, you will burn out. The Myth of Perfection in your mind will convince you it's possible to do it all, when it isn't.

If you have a lot of interests and ideas, ask yourself whether they're coming from a grounded place or a place of reacting to how other people are kicking ass and how you feel like you're not doing enough. If you can't help the barrage of ideas and plans you want to make, the key is to *sequence* instead of doing everything at once. Allow for space between plans and projects. Being scattered is the result of not feeling grounded (and not giving yourself enough self-care and rest), which only makes you feel more overwhelmed. Just as with prototyping, keep it simple and small. Start with one thing. Then do the next.

Another thing I like to use is the "idea folder." Instead of committing to and acting on an idea, give it a few days, if not a few weeks. I write out my ideas and place them in a folder labeled "Ideas." If I forget about the idea after a while, it wasn't that sustainable to begin with. If I'm still thinking about the idea weeks later, then there might be something interesting worth pursuing.

Now, I can get real with you, right? Sometimes the reason our plate is so full is that we keep putting things back on it *after* we've eliminated, delegated, or automated. Why? Because we're controlling. Plain and simple. And remember, of course you'd be controlling if you'd felt unsafe in your world since you were a little girl, unsure of whether you belonged and unsure of whether others would like you. Becoming controlling would be a very natural way to respond. I'd be surprised if you *weren't* controlling. So be gentle with yourself. This isn't another reason to dislike yourself— it's a pattern to bring into your awareness so it can begin to transform. If this is one of your primary myths, you've probably been called a "control freak" (*raises hand*).

The opposite of control and rigidity is—you guessed it—chaos and messiness. A dash of chaos is healthy in life. It's everywhere in nature. And all great creativity comes from a place of chaos. The Big Bang came from chaos. As good girls, we like to make sure all areas of our lives are sealed airtight in ziplock bags and wrapped with silk bows, but the truth is that we need some messiness in certain areas of our life in order to prioritize our needs, desires, and sanity.

Trade-offs, Heroine! Trade-offs.

At the end of the day, remind yourself that trade-offs are an inevitable part of life. For every decision we make in life, we make a trade-off. When you decide to wear the beige blouse with the speckled print, you're trading off the chambray. When you decide to focus on dating, you trade off time spent working. But the Myth of Perfection, when it's on its hyperachievement bent, makes us believe that we can be everything and do everything at one time. It's asking us to be superwomen on steroids, which is simply unsustainable. What we really must do is embrace the mess and the trade-offs and let go of the need to be everything all the time. When you're deep in your work, you might forget to brush your hair (honestly; happens to me *all the time*). When you're deep into self-care, you might make less money in your business. When you're trying to get an A+ in every area of life, you'll burn out. So try mindful chaos instead. Mindful chaos is chaos that you choose to embrace (instead of beat yourself up about) in one area of your life because you're prioritizing another.

Okay, this raises the question: How do you know whether you're making a trade-off or being a workaholic? In the previous section, I told you that some of us need to peel back from work. But now I'm telling you that trade-offs, which for you could involve ruthlessly prioritizing work, are a natural part of life. So, which one is it? Am I telling you to lean in or lean out?

This could be seen as an example of the thousands of contradictory messages women receive every day. Be beautiful, but not too beautiful; be hardworking, but not too hardworking. I'm

EMBRACE MINDFUL CHAOS

Pick one to three areas or roles in your life you're going to consciously, purposefully drop so that you don't feel bad about it. Just accept: Yup, I already knew friendships would be getting less love this year, and that's okay. Yup, I already knew that the mail would pile up for months. Write those areas down and stick them on your wall. Better to mindfully "fail" in some areas than set yourself up for greater failure by trying to do it all.

Write down three life areas you choose to mindfully let go in the next few months.

_____

_____

_____

certainly not trying to abide by this kind of patriarchal tightrope-walking double standard. It boils down to intention. Whenever we make a trade-off, it's good to go in with eyes wide open and make a conscious choice, such as "Because I'm going to work extra hard this year, I'm not going to be dating." The choice is coming from an empowered, conscious place in which you understand that sacrifices will be made to honor a commitment, dream, and priority. There is absolutely nothing wrong with that. And there's nothing wrong with consciously making work your priority. But that's different from not being sure you're in the right job, not enjoying your position, and not having gone in with your eyes wide open. In this case, you might want work–life balance but your subconscious self-sabotaging tendency to overwork (because of your contingent self-worth) is preventing you from fully experiencing it.

So the questions become the following: Do you want to be doing it? Are you conscious of the sacrifices you're making? Is your behavior aligned with your greater goals and purpose? Is the motivation underlying these goals intrinsic (e.g., the work is satisfying and you learn a lot), or is it extrinsic (e.g., you want to prove to your parents that you can do it and make them proud)? These are the questions that allow us to determine whether we're making a conscious, healthy trade-off that is breaking the Myth of Perfection or following an unhealthy pattern that is upholding that myth again and again.

Saying No

You knew we'd get here. I could have dedicated this whole book to saying no. People will try to pile things on your plate. They will punt, request, suggest, push, smack, and kick items onto your plate. So you need to set solid boundaries and appropriate expectations. You have to become your own advocate and say, "No, sorry, Mac, I won't write that memo for you."

If that sounds too difficult, I have a technique to share that I call the Focus Sandwich. In the middle of your Focus Sandwich is, well, your focus. You know I love spells, so this trick is a simple reframe that will tantalize Mac. Tell him no by saying yes to your focus (all the more reason for you to know your focus). You open and end with a great note (the gluten-free bread slices), and in the middle you have your focus (the veggie hummus). So, it sounds like this:

SAY NO

Write down a request you need to turn down because your plate is too full (oh, I'm sure you have one!) and go through the sandwich.

Positive:_____

Focus:_____

Positive:_____

Don't stop with this exercise. Send the email or text. Have the conversation. Say no by saying yes to your focus.

Positive note—"Mac, thanks for thinking of me for this." (Gratitude works wonders.)

Gooey, tasty focus—"But I'm spending my evenings with my family, who are in town this week. Family is super important to me."

Positive note—"Again, I really appreciate you giving me opportunities to step up and get more involved. You're awesome."

You can do this for anything—if someone asks for your time, energy, or money, instead of saying no, tell them what you're saying yes to. I can't go to Jamaica this year because I'm focusing on launching my Etsy store. I can't speak at your event on pickles because I'm focused on almond milk this year. I can't donate $100 to your campaign because I'm donating my funds this year to animal rights issues. Get it? Let people know what you care about, and they'll understand you're saying no to them, and they'll respect you for it. They'll be like, "Dang, this woman knows what she wants."

And if they're pissed and you experience backlash, then, fuck 'em. Or, more diplomatically, you might have misaligned priorities or an unhealthy relationship on your hands. There could be a deeper issue to look at (if this is your case, stay tuned for the Myth of Harmony). Remember, your first commitment is to thyself.

Self-Compassion

As we choose to do less, make mindful trade-offs, and say no, we'll need to love ourselves up some more. According to researcher and self-compassion expert Kristin Neff, self-compassion involves three building blocks: (1) mindfulness—staying centered and not overidentifying with the negative events in our lives; (2) common humanity—recognizing that everyone suffers, fails, and makes mistakes and that we're not alone; and (3) self-kindness, which she describes as "the tendency to be caring and understanding with oneself rather than harshly critical or judgmental, offering soothing and comfort to the self in times of suffering."[14] In other words, let's admit we're human, not superhuman like Elastigirl, and remember we're doing our best. Through my coaching work, I have found self-compassion to be a fantastic, scientifically validated practice that works wonders in countering perfectionism and chronic feelings of failure. Go ahead and try it.

 SELF-COMPASSION MEDITATION

Download and practice my free Self-Compassion Meditation, available on my website: majomeditation.com.

WHEN I WAS WORKING AT THE RESEARCH LAB AT STANFORD, I was walking down the street with a major gloomy face and crinkled forehead when an old man stopped me. Now, I've been stopped before by men who made the dreaded request "You should smile!," so I expected that was what he was going to say. But instead, he said, "If you're unhappy like this, imagine how ordinary folk feel."

I was shocked. In that moment, this man gave me some good medicine in the form of perspective. He clearly didn't think I was ordinary—which in some ways was true. Being white, thin, healthy, conventionally beautiful, one could see I was privileged. And so he broadened my frame of view in that moment—even on our worst days, most of us (especially if we're reading this book) have our basics covered and are not scrambling for food, water, housing, or medical care to make it through another day. In fact, because we're not in extreme survival mode, we can even take a moment to think about our conditioning and work to better ourselves! Relatively speaking, we're doing fine, more than fine. This isn't necessarily a reason to feel guilty but something that can help us expand our point of view. We can broaden our perspective even further, beyond society to the entire universe. As Carl Sagan once said in reflecting on our Earth from space, we are floating "on a mote of dust suspended in a sunbeam," which means you are a tiny mote on a mote.

You can also zoom out in terms of time. Think about famous folks—Genghis Khan to Joan of Arc—who changed the course of world history. How many times do you think about these people in your day? Beyond history class, probably very little, unless you're a historian. Yet they were quite significant during their lifetimes. The point is that everything changes and passes.

When we come to understand this wisdom of impermanence, we can let go. We can take risks, make mistakes, and unleash our creative potential with courage. But we can also see that we're all in this together, floating on a mote of dust in the universe. We're all on the same journey, returning to the dust pile; sorry, but it's inevitable. As too many spiritual traditions have told us by now, we belong together and separation is an illusion. When we're caught in the Myth of Perfection, we're comparing, competing, and so desperately trying to achieve and to avoid failure that we aren't allowing ourselves to be seen as we truly are—vulnerable people trying to make sense of this wild existence together. When we don't allow ourselves to be really seen, we lose our connection and belongingness to and with ourselves and others. And, let's get real, isn't connection what we're truly, deeply longing for?

Your New Toolbox

Listed here are all the tools we've explored in this chapter, along with their page numbers so you can quickly reference and practice them whenever you need to.

- Take action on your ideas and goals today (not tomorrow): **Prototyping** (see page 96).

- Share, be seen, and grow: **Vulnerability Edge Process** (see page 105).

- Unhook your worth from work: **Doing to Being Mantra** and **Nondoing Meditation** (see pages 112 and 113).

- Protect your time: **Set Your Work Boundaries Exercise** (see page 118).

- Do less: **Clearing Your Plate Process** (see page 120).

- Embrace trade-offs: **Mindful Chaos Technique** (see page 124).

- Say no: **Focus Sandwich Technique** (see page 126).

- Be kind to yourself: **Self-Compassion Meditation** (see page 128).

For further exploration and resources, including self-care rituals and meditations for the Myth of Perfection, see the appendix.

6

The Myth
of Logic

The Myth of Logic

SOUNDS LIKE

"It's best to follow my mind and intellect over my body and intuition."

LOOKS LIKE

The tendency to choose logic over intuition in decision making.

MAIN STRATEGY FOR APPROVAL

Being smart and credible.

POWERS YOU GIVE UP

Your intuition, imagination, and empathy.

WHEN MY MOM WAS TWELVE, SHE WAS SEVERELY electrocuted. She and her twin sister had been taking turns with the shower when my mom reached over with her wet hands to plug in a lamp my grandfather had temporarily placed there during renovations. As my mom buzzed on the floor, on the brink of death, her twin reached down to touch her, taking on the brunt of the electrical current. They both lay on the floor, convulsing. Meanwhile, my grandma was cooking in the kitchen when an eerie, inexplicable feeling washed over her. And then, she *just knew what to do*. My mom would tell me this story with vivid detail: "Your *abuelita* walked to the small foyer, in the opposite direction of the bathroom, and turned off the electricity to the whole house." Now, if that doesn't give you goose bumps, I don't know what will. My mom added, "If she had come to the bathroom instead, it would have been too late."

When I asked my mom *how* my grandma knew what to do, she would simply reply, "She doesn't know why she did it. She just got a bad feeling." Obviously my grandma did not use logic to determine what to do in that vital moment. I'm going to define *logic* as finding solutions through linear cause and effect and making decisions through pros and cons (I know, a very logical-sounding definition; perfect!). If she had used logic, she would have rationalized herself out of her instinct, calling it nonsense, and kept on stirring the pot as her daughters spasmed on the bathroom floor nearby. But instead she listened, without any question, to her gut. She used a completely different form of intelligence that came from within—her intuition. Our intuition is a *felt sense* about something or someone. It often whispers things to us that don't add up on paper or solutions that seem ridiculous and totally random. And yet our intuition is a form of intelligence we must learn to value as much as our logical one, which society already values. Our intuition comes from our bodies, and the good news is we all have bodies.

Yet if you were a good girl like me, it's likely that at some point while growing up, you became disconnected from your body. The first time I started wearing lip gloss, for example, was right around the time I stopped playing soccer, climbing trees, and running around barefoot in the yard with my brother. At twelve years of age, wearing lip gloss marked a final shift that had been creeping up for many years—one of being a "subject" (a vehicle through which to experience and create the world) to an "object" for boys and men.

And it's a common story. By the time a girl approaches puberty, she begins to receive comments from virtually everyone around her that her body needs to be controlled to fit into a certain standard. Advertisements, movies, and television all show unrealistic images of female beauty. We no longer see our bodies as a source of pleasure and joy, from the inside out, but see them as mounds of flesh to be looked upon, from the outside in. Many of us with stories of sexual assault (the worst form of violence on the body) are met with skepticism, deflection, and gaslighting when we tell the people whom we trust the most. We are not believed. As a way to cope with the reality of living in an abusive, misogynistic world, we form a protective rift between our heads and our bodies. Even if you haven't personally experienced major trauma or abuse, I guarantee you know a girl or woman who has. I guarantee you've received psychological blows to your body in the form of comments, rejections, and the images you saw while growing up suggesting your body is not as miraculous as she truly is.

One of the main ways our bodies speak to us, and the *key* to our intuition, is through feelings. We don't need to have proof or reasoning, or even to be able to understand how we know what we know; we just *know* it through a feeling. According to one of the grandfathers of modern psychology, William James, feelings arise first as bodily sensations, and then our brain labels them "joy," or "sadness," and creates a story about what we're experiencing.[1] Before our brain can catch up, our body is speaking to us all the time through *feelings*—think arm hairs that stand up, tingles that run up and down our spine, a sinking gut, or how our joints know when a storm is coming.

But in the patriarchy, the message we've been told is simple: feelings and emotions are a weakness. We shame boys and men by calling them "pussies" and "girls" (as if being a female is the worst insult ever) when they express sadness or anxiety. We shame women, telling them they're crazy, hysterical, and overreacting to forms of dominance, aggression, and violence. While men in the patriarchy are emasculated, women are defeminized. One of the easiest ways to defeminize us is to shame us for our sensitivity.

Hysteria was once an *actual* medical condition invented by male doctors who didn't know what to do with women's feelings and the truth they reveal to us. Labeling women "hysterical" made it easier to control them. You could conveniently put them in an asylum and dismiss their stories (of sexual abuse, for example) as crazy. Or just call them witches. As psychiatrist Julie Holland wrote in a wonderful *New York Times* op-ed, "Women's emotionality is a sign of health, not disease; it is a source of power. But we are under constant pressure to restrain our emotional lives. We have been taught to apologize for our tears, to suppress our anger and to fear being called hysterical."[2]

While hysteria is, thankfully, a medical diagnosis of the past, we're still living with its consequences. My mom told me a harrowing story about going to the doctor multiple times, telling them about a sharp, unbearable pain in her side. Every doctor told her there was nothing wrong with her and wrote off her pain (I'm sure it didn't help that she's an immigrant with an accent). One evening she had a strong intuition that her problem was serious, so she went to another doctor, who similarly wrote her off, but she insisted that she wasn't leaving until he did more tests. He relented, and they discovered she had a severely inflamed gallbladder and needed emergency surgery. My father, a doctor himself, was in disbelief. "If you hadn't insisted, you might not be here today," he said.

A friend told me a similar story of her sister, who was told by multiple doctors that she was suffering from hypochondria, until they finally diagnosed her with multiple sclerosis (MS). "My sister could have been diagnosed and treated earlier if they had believed her," my friend told me. "She lived only an hour away from the Mayo Clinic, which is world-renowned for treating MS."

Is it surprising that if the world around us, including modern medicine, doesn't believe in our feelings and pain, we begin to doubt ourselves? In the face of ongoing skepticism and shaming, we've been trained to second-guess ourselves instead of trusting our bodies. This is by far the biggest consequence when we buy into the Myth of Logic—we could *die*. When we doubt ourselves, we step away from being our own advocates in a medical system that may very well not listen to us. We get caught in the disempowering cycle—we deny our feelings, so we get sick, and then when we get sick, we are not believed (and we in turn doubt ourselves), so we deny our feelings even more and get sicker.

Besides the dangerous potential of disease and death when we don't listen to our bodies, when we're under the spell of the Myth of Logic, we also risk making disempowering life decisions. When we follow logic over intuition, we marry the person or take the job that makes sense on paper instead of what feels true in our gut. I've seen this play out for numerous clients who overthink and agonize over decisions, not only because they're afraid of getting it wrong but also because they have no idea what yes and no feel like in their bodies. They barely feel their bodies! Through years of good girl conditioning, they've lost their ability to feel the subtle yet important difference between fear and intuition. This ability is not only a basic survival instinct; it's a basic navigational skill we need if we want to live a fulfilled life.

Finally, when we follow the Myth of Logic, we squander one of our superpowers—our imagination. Under this myth, we don't allow ourselves to be generative, and we end up creating from a place that is mediocre, uninventive, and stale. We need our intuition and bodies to create with true instinct and power. Like intuition, creativity is a complement to logic we can't abandon.

If we want to give our gifts to the world, we need to break the spell of the Myth of Logic and unapologetically own the full range of our emotional and creative intelligence as women. We can do that by reclaiming our feelings and our imaginations. Let's look at some ways to do that.

Reclaiming Feelings

The first step in strengthening our intuitive intelligence is to reclaim our feelings. We need to learn to resensitize and un-numb ourselves. Let's return to our first design thinking–inspired mindset: *seek deeper understanding* through empathy, particularly emotional empathy. Emotional empathy is the backbone of human-centered design, and at its core it's what distinguishes design from simply building things. If a designer isn't able to deeply understand how and what other people *feel*, there's no way she can design better services, products, or experiences for them. When something is well designed, its form and function trigger satisfying feelings—such as delight, joy, ease, or relaxation—in us. Since designers are problem-solvers and want their designs to conjure positive feelings, they spend a lot of time understanding negative feelings, especially frustration, anger, and irritability. The best designers understand emotional "pain points."

How can we design the best possible lives for ourselves if we ignore our own pain points? As good girls, too many of us learn to put on a happy face and pretend it's all okay, when deep down we know something isn't right. We need to allow ourselves to feel everything, especially the *hard* feelings. As author and researcher Brené Brown says, "we can't selectively numb emotion."[3] When we don't allow ourselves to feel pain, we miss out on the opportunity to design our lives for more joy.

Nowhere was this phenomenon more clear than it was with my client Ines, a twenty-nine-year-old Russian American copywriter whose marriage was falling apart. As we sat down during our first session, I could see she was doing everything in her power to keep herself together, avoiding the subject of her husband completely. When I finally asked about their relationship, her lower lip quivered and she started weeping. Overwhelmed and embarrassed by the sudden flood of tears, she quickly wiped them away and kept repeating "Anyway" while U-turning the conversation back to her job search. I knew the strategy all too well, as I'd used it multiple times before: staying in my mind (and its many rationalizations) as a way to avoid the discomfort and pain coursing through my body. But I wouldn't let her turn away. It was uncomfortable, but I sensed she needed to feel her pain (i.e., self-empathy) for the next phase of her life to unfold.

"Let's sit with this," I said. "And get curious." (Something both design thinking and mindfulness have in common is *curiosity*.)

She reluctantly closed her eyes, tears streaming down her face.

"What are you feeling?" I asked.

"Sad. Confused."

"Ahh," I said. "Where do you feel it?"

"In my chest."

"What does it feel like?"

"Pain," she said.

"Can you describe it without giving it a label? What are its qualities?"

She paused and took a deep breath. "Boiling, tight . . . unpleasant."

139

"Let's keep feeling it," I told her. "See if you can dive into the sensations a bit more."

"Argh, okay," she sighed, realizing there was no escape button that would parachute her out of the session. She would be facing the very feelings she had been avoiding for so long. But after a minute or so, her eyebrows, which had been tightly knit, began to relax.

"What's happening now?" I asked her, genuinely curious about the new moment emerging before my eyes.

"The pain . . ." she said. "It's softer now . . ."

Through mindful observation, her uncomfortable feelings *moved*. We both took a deep exhale. Starting in this moment, Ines was able to come to terms with her unmet needs in the relationship and her realization that *something* needed to change in order for her to live her most authentic, powerful life. If Ines hadn't allowed herself to feel her pain, she would have kept humming along for weeks, months, and years denying the truth to herself. Her courage to look within and *seek deeper understanding* was what allowed her to take action and redesign her life, which included moving out and landing a new job that would enable her to financially support herself.

Like Ines, we can learn to un-numb ourselves through the practice of mindful attention and observation. *Mindfulness* is the practice of directing our awareness to the ever-changing thoughts and feelings inside us. Instead of slapping a label on our feelings, mindfulness invites us to feel the sheer rawness of their physical sensations (i.e., discomfort or pain) in the body. Stemming from Buddhism, mindfulness is a powerful practice that has been validated by numerous scientific studies. But you don't need a study to know it works. You simply need your experience. Next time you're feeling negative, take a moment to pause, close your eyes, and simply observe the sensations in your body, especially in your belly, chest, and throat. Close your eyes and dive into the internal spaces of those three body areas. Common sensations might include clenching, heaviness, dullness, or burning, among many others. As you stay curious and open about what you observe, you may notice your feelings move instead of stagnate. This is a basic beginner's *mindfulness practice*, something you can come back to as you need to (I include it as a tool in your toolbox at the end of this chapter).

As we practice mindfulness, we naturally become more aware of our many strategies for escaping and numbing our difficult feelings. How do you cope with these feelings of loneliness, grief, or anxiety? What do you reach for? When I feel very moody, anxious, or lonely, I like to shop (anyone else?). But there are plenty of other potential addictions and endless distractions around—food, work, sex, alcohol, technology, social media, whatever will allow us not to feel what we're feeling. What's your poison? Notice your coping strategies and how certain physical sensations in the body lead you to self-medicate.

Mindfulness requires us to slow down. If you're rushing from one thing to the next, your feelings won't have the breathing room they need to be fully felt. Many clients fear they feel too much, but that's not the problem. The problem is they don't give themselves the space to feel all the way. How can you create space for yourself to feel more? For me, it's drinking a cup of warm tea in the morning—that's it, simply putting a few leaves in a cup and watching them unfurl. It's a time when I can take in and really process all the things that are happening to me. A doctor and founder of a health-care startup once told me that for her it was yoga. "Yoga was a moment of waking up to right now and realizing I had this huge concrete wall [between my head and body]," she told me. "In many ways, I was low-grade abusing myself—living on crappy food, not exercising, partying at night, being in a crappy relationship with a crappy boyfriend at the time—and yoga was a moment of stillness when I started listening." For others, it's a meditation practice or a flow activity (e.g., weaving, hiking) in which we can feel all our feels instead of distracting, numbing, and "low-grade abusing" ourselves. If we want to feel our feelings, we must slow down and go inward.

Mindfulness also teaches us to trust our feelings, which means no self-judgment. We don't shame a tree for its leaves falling one day and flowers blossoming the next day, do we? We simply say that's what a tree does and is. When we're under the Myth of Logic, we try to rationalize ourselves out of our feelings or tell ourselves that we shouldn't be feeling that way. But feelings (and certainly moods) don't require an explanation; they simply are, exactly like a tree or the weather.

Searching for the why and the cause is trying to apply a logical, fixed approach to a fluid and ever-changing phenomenon. I'm talking about the kind of questioning that gets you down on your knees pleading with the skies, "Why?!" It's the kind of *why* that hooks us when we're down. When we ask "Why do I feel this way?" we are sending ourselves a message that we shouldn't be feeling this way. Plus, the why is often far too complex and invisible for us even to attempt to understand. The planets? Our hormones? Years of built-up trauma? Somebody else's feelings we've caught on to? Asking why also leads us into a problem-solving mind-set (how do I get rid of this feeling as soon as possible?) because we assume that if we know the cause, we can eliminate the feeling, which is not always the case. It might give us the illusion of control in a situation in which we have very little, but it only makes things worse. Compulsive worry about the causes, and consequences, of our feelings is called *rumination*, and it only leads us into a deeper hole. In fact, women are 70 percent more likely than men to develop depression throughout their lifetimes.[4] In over two decades of research on gender differences in depression, the late Susan Nolen-Hoeksema, chair of Yale University's Department of Psychology, found that girls and women ruminate more than boys and men and, as a result, are more likely to amplify their mood and stay in a rut.[5] The research speaks for itself: it's way better to let feelings move through you fully, mindfully, and swiftly, without glossing over them, than to dwell on them for too long.

Buddhists have their own term for rumination: *the second arrow*. We can't control the first arrow—say, a stressful life event or a terrible sadness that suddenly lands on us—but we can control the second arrow, which is our response to the first. We feel angry at X, we feel sad because Y, and that's 100 percent valid and okay. Don't judge yourself for feeling the way you do. When we stay open instead of judgmental, we allow ourselves to receive the information we need to navigate our lives with greater wisdom.

There's no doubt that mindfulness helps us process our feelings, but sometimes we need a more active release, especially if we've been taught to overregulate our feelings. During a recent consultation call, a woman shared with me, "I spend a lot of time with engineers and researchers, and I find myself hiding my emotions and managing how I talk because I don't want my co-workers to feel my negativity or think I'm being 'dramatic,' you know?" She went on to say that her extreme "emotion management" isn't just a strategy she uses at work but one she also uses with her girlfriends. "Oh, I often bite my tongue," she told me, "because I don't want them to think I'm mad at them." How do you think this woman felt at the end of the day? Exhausted and drained. That stoic or smiling mask takes a lot of energy to maintain!

It also creates major problems. In Eastern medicine, disease is seen as the accumulation of toxins and negative beliefs. The key word here is *accumulation*. When we don't release feelings, they "back up" and create blockages, which eventually lead to mental and physical imbalance. In our fear of looking crazy, we suppress feelings, and then they rupture, only fulfilling the prophecy— people label us as crazy and we may even feel crazy. We can break this cycle by releasing our feelings in safe, healthy containers that we design for ourselves. We don't have to dwell quietly on our negative feelings because that's what good girls do. We can be loud and expressive, either in privacy or with trained professionals and people we trust. In our next myth, the Myth of Harmony, we'll talk about how to be more vulnerable with the people who are triggering us by having those long-overdue difficult conversations, but for now, I'm sharing some of my favorite ways to release feelings on our own.

Cry

It's not uncommon to hear a client tell me, "I hate it when I cry," or try to explain away their feelings with "I have no real reason to cry." Crying is vulnerable. And the patriarchy doesn't like it when we cry (except when it's your birthday, when you can cry if you want to), and so, naturally, we don't like it when we cry. It's helpful to reflect: What were you told as a child about your crying? Were you called a crybaby? Were you told, "It isn't such a big deal," or asked, "Why are you crying?" Your tears are a form of power, and perhaps they have made others uncomfortable in your past, but you can reclaim this power for yourself moving forward.

Tears tell us when something is moving us, when something is not all right with us, or when we're overwhelmed. They're telling us how we *feel* about a situation. And if they are communicating how we feel, they are a part of the intuitive intelligence I've been describing.

So own your tears, and break down if you need to. A client and I devised a daily challenge: she would lie on her bed for at least ten minutes (she could go longer, but ten minutes is enough time to overcome mental resistance to doing the behavior) and let herself feel and cry for however long she needed. Given she had so many feels, this was super cathartic and therapeutic for her. She noticed a boost in her mood the following day, and she had way more energy to focus on her most meaningful work. Ask me how many times I've cried while writing this book, from both glory and pain. The answer is *just enough*.

Scream, Punch, Kick, and Throw

Once my husband spent time with a female friend and, afraid of how I'd respond, waited days to tell me about it. As he feared, I was filled with jealousy, mistrust, and full-on rage (there's back-story I won't go into right now, but my reaction felt justified). We both could tell I needed to physically process the emotions I was feeling, so I asked him to stack and hold a few dense pillows to his chest, and then I proceeded to kick the shit out of those pillows. I think I must have kicked for thirty minutes straight, and my husband stood there, holding on for his dear life. I commend him for holding space for my rage with such grace. For you, doing this may look like screaming into a pillow, or going to a kickboxing class or gym or to a river's edge where you can throw some rocks as far as you can. Get out that aggression and anger. Be fierce. No shame. Let it circulate and breathe.

Forgive

Who do you need to forgive? Some of the gnarliest emotions that are stuck in our bodies can dissolve through forgiveness. We don't forgive for others; we forgive for ourselves. Blame and resentment erode us from the inside out. Think about the different people you are in relationship with. Start with your parents and primary caregivers. How about other family members? Move on to your teachers. What about your friends, your significant other, or even former friends and lovers? Forgiveness is a key part of releasing toxic feelings that might be building up in your system and no longer serving you. Who do you need to forgive?

Dance

Since emotions are stuck in the body, one of the most brilliant ways to let them out is to dance. Play your favorite track and dance until you sweat and get your heart rate up. Dance when nobody's watching, or go to a safe space to dance with others. If dance doesn't resonate, sweat through other forms of exercise and physical exertion, like running, cycling, or high-intensity training. The point is: move your body.

Journal

One of the surest, quickest ways to externalize your feelings is to journal by hand or type with ruthless abandon. Whenever I have so many feels about something but life keeps going at its frenetic pace, externalizing on the page both allows me to acknowledge my feelings and gives me the perspective that feelings are like waves that come and go, so it's important to let them flow. I love making quick and dirty "inner critic lists" where I list out all the negative beliefs I'm having about myself that are usually coupled with my feelings of anxiety, failure, and overwhelm. I take only a few minutes on these lists, but I always feel better when I externalize the thoughts either emerging from or leading to my feelings, and then I move on (that's key; otherwise, you're ruminating). Other insights might follow too, as experienced by a client who shared, "I wrote out a bunch of feelings towards my parents, and that helped a lot. At the end of the day, I realize I can't change them; I can only improve myself."

Honor Your Cycle

Our feelings and moods can sometimes relate to our menstrual cycles. The patriarchy pretty much hates menstruation, so many of us develop an unhealthy relationship with our periods. We learn to utterly despise them, and if we could wish them away with magic wands, we would. We experience shame around our cycles. I know that during most of my teen years I felt embarrassed about the uncontrollable moodiness I felt during my luteal (premenstrual) phase, fearing that if I got "too emotional," my friends (and especially my guy friends and boyfriends) would label me as crazy, so I kept everything low-key when I was having my period and tried to fly under the radar. I basically learned it's not okay to be a woman.

An easy way to become friendly with your cycle is to track it, so you can learn when to lean into your feelings hygiene. Since I tend to have more negative feelings and thoughts before I bleed, I write plenty of those inner critic lists right around this time. I've also found it helpful to expand my view of menstruation by learning how other cultures view it. In their book *Blood Magic: The Anthropology of Menstruation*, cultural anthropologists Alma Gottlieb and Thomas Buckley explore menstruation around the world and suggest that not all cultures see it as taboo, or cursed, as has been claimed by many earlier ethnographers. In the case of a northwestern California indigenous tribe, the Yurok, for example, a menstruating woman would isolate herself in a lodge, not because it was shameful but because she was at "the height of her powers" and this time should be focused toward the "'accumulation' of spiritual energy."[6] The authors wrote that Yurok women also went to the "sacred moon pond" to perform purifying bathing rituals, and "through such practice women came to 'see that the earth has her own moontime,' a recognition that made one both 'stronger' and 'proud' of one's menstrual cycle."[7] Maybe one day we'll get there (and by all means, if you find a sacred moon pond, go be witchy), but for now, we can begin to reorient our relationship with our cycles by becoming more mindful of them through conscious tracking, as well as honoring and releasing our feelings in healthy ways during parts of our cycle that need it the most.

EXPRESS YOUR FEELINGS

Look back at these strategies for reclaiming your feelings and choose one or two that you can commit to doing or trying for the first time this week. Schedule a dedicated container of time for whichever forms of expression you choose. Then debrief in your journal what the experience was like.

Developing Your Intuition

The mindful observation of our bodily sensations can help us process difficult feelings, and it can also help us access our inner wisdom when we need to make key life decisions. One of my clients, Vansha, a forty-three-year-old software product manager, received a job offer from a swanky startup in London. Under the Myth of Logic, she made a list of pros and cons in an effort to decide if she should take the job. It was clear that the pros outweighed the cons, but the cons felt like pebbles in her shoe. Something (but what?) didn't feel right. Vansha couldn't put her finger on it. Practically speaking, she should take the job. It was high-paying and checked all the other boxes as well. I realized we needed to create a practice of listening to what a yes feels like and what a no feels like *in her body*. It involved going inward instead of searching for answers outside herself. I asked Vansha to close her eyes and guided her through a visualization of working in London.

"What's happening in your body?"

"I feel heavy, almost sleepy."

"Do you feel expanded or contracted?"

149

She paused to listen a bit more. "Contracted. Definitely contracted."

I asked her to elaborate. What did contraction feel like, exactly? She mentioned that her throat had tightened up and there was a pinch in her belly. As we sat with the feeling, she began to express her uneasiness with the team, how when she entered the company's office, her body had immediately tensed up. We had our answer. London was *not* her next move. It was a simple exercise, but her body was handing her the wisdom she needed.

Through mindfulness, we can tap into this powerful, deeper form of intelligence. Next time you're feeling uncertain about a decision, get quiet, close your eyes, and listen to your body's cues. Visualize a scenario in which you answer yes to the decision—how does your body respond? Imagine a scenario in which you answer no to the decision—how does your body respond? You can begin to record and learn your cues, which are different for each of us. Let's call this the *Body's Yes Versus No Technique*, and you can come back to it as needed. It's also included in your toolbox at the end of the chapter.

When a decision is a no for me, my breath feels more stuck and shallow, while a yes often means a deep sigh of relief or a feeling that my breath is circulating through my limbs more freely. It can be as simple as expansion, in which your body relaxes and feels as if it's swelling or getting bigger, versus contraction, in which your shoulders tighten and you feel as if you're shrinking. Slow down, pay attention, and practice. All the wisdom in the world you need is right at home, in your body.

Awe Versus Fear

I'll be the first to admit—expansion doesn't *always* feel comfortable. It can feel scary, sometimes even terrifying. In recent decades, psychologists have studied awe, a complex emotion we feel in the face of beauty, possibility, and vastness. You know, what you feel when you look up at the stars and contemplate how freakin' big the universe is and how itty-bitty you are. Experiences of awe make us question what we thought we knew and revise our stories about the world, which is why it's in direct opposition to the Myth of Logic. In fact, in one study, researchers Michelle Shiota and colleagues found that people who are "uncomfortable with ambiguity" (cough—*logical*) report experiencing awe less often than do people who are okay with not knowing and with revising their own mental structures.[8] Makes sense!

Awe is a vulnerable emotion because it requires you to feel how small you are (and how little you know), which means not everybody is up for it. But that's a shame, because I believe *one of the ways your body speaks to you is through awe*. The confusing part is that awe can feel like fear in the body. Our nervous system is made up of two branches: the parasympathetic nervous system (PNS) and the sympathetic nervous system (SNS). The PNS is responsible for the relaxation response, what we feel when we're safe, grazing the grasses, resting, and digesting. The SNS, on the other hand, is responsible for what we feel when we're afraid on the most basic, instinctual level; typical responses include fight, flee, or freeze. Some people call this "lizard brain" fear. The SNS also stimulates a faster breath pace (and heart rate) and, in many animals, the shivers—a classic fear response. Though awe triggers the PNS more so than the SNS, it *can* quicken or suspend the breath (i.e., gasping), cause goose bumps, and trigger a freeze response (e.g., jaw dropping, eyes widening). Obviously there's a difference between your eyes getting wider because you're watching the northern lights and the blank stare of a terrified deer caught

in headlights, but you can see why your mind might get a bit confused and think, *Run or stay, run or stay?*

Let's circle back to Vansha. Imagine that she visualized taking
the job in London and suddenly her body locked up and got very
still. Imagine she whispered that she wasn't sure she could do the
job, and though she's wanted to live in London since she was a
little girl, she has this sense of "Who am I to uproot my life and
go to London at age forty-three?" Imagine tears had fallen on her
cheeks and her breath had become suspended and then a little
faster. Vansha might have thought, "Well, I guess I'm not supposed
to go to London! Clearly, my body and feelings don't want me
to." But in fact, Vansha would have been experiencing awe, which
would have been a *Yes, yes, yes, go, go, go.*

We need to learn to disentangle awe from fear. Lizard-brain
fear tells us a legitimate no, while awe tells us something far bigger is calling us forward (which is scary!). Awe tells us that the
business we want to start or the country we want to move to feels
true. Researchers Dacher Keltner and Jonathan Haidt propose that
awe has many flavors: "beauty-based," which is when you're in
front of a gorgeous piece of art or landscape; "ability-based," when
you are confronted with someone's gifts; and "virtue-based," when
you see someone displaying a virtue you admire.[9] Awe is a mix of
seeing beauty, gifts, and virtues around you. Why can't we experience awe when we touch upon our own beauty, gifts, and virtues?
When we sense a new, wild possibility for our lives? If we allow
ourselves, we can learn to feel the awe of our own future potential.

If you want to break the spell of the Myth of Logic, allow yourself to feel awe more often, and pay attention to the physical sensations. Put yourself in front of breathtaking landscapes and pieces
of art, let time slow down, feel your sense of self diminish, feel

that you're plugged in to the universe, experience the vastness, and sit with the mystery of it all. Feel what *that's* like in your body, and take note: goose bumps, chills, tingles, tears, suspension of breath, possibility, possibility, possibility . . . The more you can read these cues, the better you'll get at distinguishing awe from lizard-fear and following where your intuition takes you.

The Wise Woman Within

One way to get in touch with our bigness is to visualize ourselves thirty or forty years from now when we become (hopefully) a wise old woman. I love guiding clients through this visualization when I feel they're caught up in rationalizing a decision instead of intuiting one. The idea is that deep inside you is a wise woman, and she's waiting for you to ask her for guidance. I like to think of my wise woman within as a crone who's been there, done that, seen the world, is ruthlessly honest, and doesn't have time to sugarcoat the truth for me. Melting into ashes is right around the corner, so she's going to give it to me straight. Think of your wise woman as a personification of your intuition. She's the internal compass that pulls—not pushes—you toward your truth. With pushing energy, we have striving and forcing. That's how we feel when we're overthinking and ruminating about our options. With pulling energy, we have ease, effortlessness, and trust. When we get clear with the wise woman within, we move from pushing to pulling energy. She begins to pull us forward toward our most authentic self. And we organically grow into her. Each woman's wise woman within looks different, sounds different, and goes by a different name, but she's a powerful, often overlooked inner resource to turn to for some guidance and clarity. My wise woman has told me to laugh more, to focus on my creativity, and to come into deeper self-acceptance. She is a beacon for my inner truth. Take some time to visualize yours and see what truth she holds for you.

WISE WOMAN WITHIN MEDITATION

If you're interested in getting in touch with your wise woman within, practice the free Wise Woman Within Meditation available on my website here: majomeditation.com.

Reclaiming Imagination

Reclaiming our emotions is such an important, powerful way to lean into our body's intuition. Another way to access what feels truly right for us is to reclaim our imagination. We'll define *imagination* as the act of forming mental images, symbols, and experiences that are new or have never existed and that aren't what we're experiencing in "reality." With Vansha, I invited her to imagine her life in London, and that gave us clues about how she truly felt about the situation. With the wise woman within, I suggested you imagine yourself decades into the future as a crone archetype—a personification of your wisdom—in order to gain fresh insight into your current situation.

Our imaginations are powerful and can create real changes in our physical state. Like intuition, imagination emerges from our inner landscape, and in addition to helping us understand ourselves, it's a gift that underpins most, if not all, creative and visionary thought. Even Einstein said, "Imagination is more important than knowledge. For knowledge is limited to all we now know and understand, while imagination embraces the entire world, and all there ever will be to know and understand."

As little girls, we were incredibly imaginative. By age four and five, children engage in make-believe and pretend play, assuming an identity, imitating, dramatizing, and assigning new meanings to objects, as when a shoe becomes a phone. We believe in magic, and we create magic. We imagine freely.

By our late teens, most of us have had any sense of wonder, magic, awe, and imagination beaten out of us by the world around us. We collect what Brené Brown calls "creativity scars."[10] We don't make the cut for the talent show. Our older brother doesn't listen to us sing. A friend tells us we'll never know how to draw. The neighbor pokes fun at our eccentric gingerbread house. You get it. We begin to believe we aren't creative. We no longer engage our imagination. Our schools, our parents, and society at large reward us when we follow the more logical subjects, like science and mathematics.

The patriarchy privileges logic above all else, making our imagination a kind of afterthought. In his book *A Whole New Mind: Why Right-Brainers Will Rule the Future*, author Daniel Pink argues that our broader culture tends to prize "L-Directed Thinking"—a type of thinking related to the left hemisphere of the brain, which is linear, literal, and analytical. On the other hand, "R-Directed Thinking"—a type of thinking related to the right hemisphere of the brain, which is holistic, contextual, and aesthetic (e.g., creative)— is "shortchanged by organizations, and neglected in schools."[11] Nowhere is this neglect more obvious than in schools. All across the world, schools focus on beefing up the L-Directed Thinking. Take a look at the hierarchy of school subjects—mathematics and sciences are at the top, while humanities and arts are at the bottom. I'm all for getting more girls and women into STEM (sciences, technology, engineering, and mathematics) fields, but I prefer the power of STEAM—adding in the *A* for arts—even more. Creativity is the backbone of innovation, so we can't leave it out. If you're laboring under the Myth of Logic, you probably fell for the idea that "hard" fields like sciences were better than "soft" fields like arts, but are they? Don't we need both?

Let's reclaim our imaginations and make the best use of the right side of our brains.

Your Inner Artist

My inner artist's name is Leela, and she lives in a human-size cocoon in the woods. I'm not kidding. I created this artist alter ego (as well as her giant papier-mâché cocoon) as part of a final assignment for a design aesthetics class in grad school. Leela is a daydreaming mystical elf who collects branches, leaves, garbage, lace, bird wings, and anything else she can find and pastes them onto the translucent walls of her cocoon. She makes no logical sense. She is simply play, feeling, and instinct. She is a lover of beauty. For the longest time, Leela was a part of myself that I completely disowned and, honestly, was kind of afraid of! Would she "go off the deep end" and never come back to be a "normal" person in society? Would she be deemed crazy and ostracized for life?

After collecting so many "creativity scars" over the years and bolstering our analytic minds, many good girls are asking the same questions or are even feeling completely disconnected from their inner artists. We think we're not artistic or creative when deep down, we are. Suspend any judgment and disbelief for a moment, and entertain the possibility that you have an inner artist—your own Leela—dying for some airtime. What would it be like to let her create freely? What would it be like to give her the respect she deserves?

 ## NAME YOUR INNER ARTIST

Grab your journal and let's do some free-writing around your inner artist. Keep your journal open because soon we'll continue this exercise with her opposing archetype, the inner skeptic.

- Write down five words to describe your inner artist. (Mine are *wild, natural, enchanted, mischievous,* and *elfish*).

- Where does your inner artist gather the most inspiration from? What are her sources of interest and curiosity? It's totally okay if these curiosities feel unrelated to your profession or what you've done in the past.

- If your inner artist were a person, what would she or he look like? Where would she or he live?

- Choose one of your five descriptors and give your inner artist an empowering name. I already told you my inner artist's name is Leela. Feel free to use a first and last name, or go mononym style like Madonna. Keep in mind that when we name something, we have more power to recognize it when it comes up, which is useful in evoking an archetype (as we want with our inner artist) but also in creating more distance from one (as we will want with our inner skeptic).

An obvious way to unleash your inner artist is to create images in whatever ways make sense for you: paint, ink, chalk, pencil. You can even use your own body, creating shapes and forms with your body and seeing what they feel like. Take some paint, splash it against a canvas, and see what shapes, forms, and patterns emerge. Go beyond verbal language and into the space of imagery.

If creating images or "art" feels way out of your comfort zone (though who came here to be comfortable?), start small and make a mood board. Designers use mood boards as a way to capture the visual essence or point of view of their ideas through a combination and composition of images and symbols. Mood boards also help expand our minds and broaden our concepts of what's possible by making connections. Suddenly we're pasting a parrot beside a water bottle and that triggers a memory, which triggers an idea, which becomes a story, and the adventure continues.

 MAKE A MOOD BOARD

This is taking the preceding exercise one step further in bringing your inner artist to life. From the point of view of your inner artist, cut up some magazine images, or print out photographs from your phone or computer, and make a mood board around your favorite color. You can even collect objects around you or in nature, or take photographs of things that capture your inner artist's eye. Though I recommend using your hands and getting tactile, if you want to use a digital tool, try Instagram or Pinterest (you can make private accounts and boards so no one will see it if you prefer).

Your Inner Skeptic

Have you noticed that as we get older, we get more skeptical about life? Every inner artist has an inner skeptic lurking in the shadows. The inner skeptic is the part of us that seems to *always* poop on our own party, right when we're finally having some fun and finger painting on the bathroom mirror. Some people call this part of ourselves the inner judge or inner critic, but I have found that neither of those descriptors captures the kind of skepticism (and even cynicism) that the Myth of Logic breeds. Creating art means opening ourselves up to magic, wonder, and awe, and our inner skeptics naturally want to tell us how they feel when we decide to let go and unleash our messy (and, let's get real, *ugly*) creativity. What are some of the thoughts of your inner skeptic when she shuts you down? Here are a few I've heard from my clients and their inner skeptics over the years when they start getting more creative.

- This isn't practical.

- This is way too cheesy.

- How will this solve my problems?

- I'm not sure creativity exists!

- That isn't highbrow enough.

- Ew.

- Did you see the cover art of the *New Yorker* this week? So. Much. Better.

NAME YOUR INNER SKEPTIC

It's time to reflect on our inner skeptics to understand what might be draining energy from our inner artists.

- Write down five words to describe your inner skeptic. (Mine are *cynical, rational, verbose, tense,* and *serious.*)

- Where do you think your inner skeptic came from? Think back to the main cultures and its authority figures we talked about in chapter 1: family, school, religion, and pop culture.

- If your inner skeptic were a person, what would she or he look like?

- Choose one of your descriptors and give your inner skeptic a disarming first and last name. Choose a name that is a bit funny and lighthearted, like Cynical Cynthia, Professor Penelope, or Queen Questioner. Alliterations work wonders, and so do titles like Lady, Madame, Mrs., and the like. The humorous name helps diffuse the power these inner skeptics have over us so that we can't take them too seriously.

Play and Games

Another way to break away from your inner skeptic is to simply play more games. When you were a little girl, odds are you laughed and smiled way more than you do now. Childlike playfulness came naturally to you. As adults, we play significantly less, but science has already shown how laughter and humor are really good for our physical and mental well-being (but you don't really need me to cite a study for that, do you?). You have felt the benefits of laughter in your body—the feeling of sheer aliveness, the invigoration, and the boundless joy.

When I go home to Argentina for multiple weeks over the holidays, I play endless board and card games with my extended family. There is something so multigenerational, deeply nourishing, and wholesome about playing board games with my family. I wouldn't trade it for the world. Games generate creativity. Comedians and performing artists have been using improvisation and improv games forever to create sketches, scenes, and scripts. In qualitative interviews with researchers, adults who regularly practiced improv shared how pretend play boosts their creative confidence, specifically their ability to trust their actions, speak more freely, bounce back from mistakes and failures, and come up with a wider range of new solutions to problems.[12] These findings don't surprise me. The Stanford d.school has offered classes on improv for this very reason—it engenders the kind of imagination we need to brainstorm, play around, tinker, and try things. Improv is all about suspending our inner skeptic and letting our imagination take over in a safe and often supportive and communal space.

For many years, I led a women's leadership circle, and at the end of every circle, we played imaginary games. In one game, I would circle the ladies up and pretend there was a giant cauldron in the middle of the circle and we would all stir the "goo" in the cauldron like a bunch of witches. "Let's pretend this is our cauldron, and we're creating a spell. We can put whatever we want in here, and every time we toss something in we have to cackle like witches do." I would encourage them not to think at all, but in a popcorn style, toss a strange, ridiculous object into the "pot." When I first did this process, the women were reluctant and a bit skeptical, probably thinking I was a weirdo, which was fine (*weird* comes from the word *wyrd*, which actually means wise—so there). But after two minutes, they got super into it. There was no grand purpose except pure, fun play! We would do this for about ten minutes, giggling like little girls and *mwihihi*-ing like witches (my job here is done). After playing this game, women told me, they felt refreshed and totally awake for the late-night drive home.

Dream Work

Once I had a dream in which a young woman was trying to record a podcast, but whenever she played back the recording, it was blank. Her voice was gone. I found out in my dream that the young woman was a ghost and had died through a tragic drowning off the shores of Muir Beach a few years prior. She was voiceless now. I woke up wondering if a woman who once lived in the house I was renting had drowned. When I asked my landlady, she looked at me and plainly stated, "Dreams tell us about our own psyches. How are you not expressing your voice?" Touché. Clearly, my landlady had done some dream work. I paused and sat with her question. It was true; while I used to love to sing, I hadn't sung in a long time, too caught up in work and life (Myth of Perfection).

Characters in our dreams are part of our own psyche. Who was the young woman within me? Dreams are part of the non-rational, and because of that, they give us clues about the deeper, difficult to access, and difficult to admit to ourselves, desires of the soul and body. After the dream, I picked up my guitar and wrote a beautiful song. I was filled with energy again and realized I couldn't afford to let my voice die. Dreams are part of our deeper intelligence, and they seldom use words, speaking instead in symbols, which is why they're so connected to creativity and artistry. I encourage you to pay attention to your dreams, and one great way to do that is by keeping a dream journal.

 ## START A DREAM JOURNAL

Choose a dedicated journal for recording your dreams that stays beside your bed and doesn't travel with you or have other purposes. The moment you wake up, record your dreams (don't wait; otherwise you will forget). Once you have your dream written down, play around with symbol associations. To make a symbol association, look at all the major objects and characters in your dreams—the car, the bird, the old woman, the bed, the Virgin Mary statue—and then write down all the quick associations (first words that come to your mind) with each of those nouns. For example, "When I think of car, what first comes to mind is . . . steel, Ford, man, progress."

Of course, you *could* look up the "universal" dream meanings behind various symbols, but what's more interesting is to understand the association you have with a specific symbol or object, because after all, it's emerging from *your* psyche. Next, "mad-lib" it by replacing the nouns of your dream. From there, you'll start to see deeper meanings and patterns emerge. The scene in which you saw a snake encircling a car could mean that your sexuality is larger and more powerful than your progress, for example. You can play around with different directions and situations to see what rings true. There's truly no right or wrong way to do dream interpretation. It's a creative process that involves your full participation.

Beyond interpreting dreams, another useful exercise is *scrying*, which comes from several occult traditions and means reading forms in a reflective surface, as a fortune teller does in her crystal ball. There are many ways to scry. You can scry by watching the different shapes of tea leaves unfurl in water. If not tea, look at coffee or cacao sediments and see if any shapes are waiting at the bottom of your cup. You can throw a string onto a table and observe the different ways it lands. You can watch clouds drifting through the sky and read the messages there too. You can read the shadows of plants and leaves against a wall at sunrise, twilight, or dusk or under the moon. There are so many ways to read the shapes of life around you, to follow the images of your life.

If you're a good girl under the Myth of Logic and find yourself skeptical and cynical about magic, I invite you to remember two key factors of your power: your feelings and your imagination. Sit with these feelings and let them express. Listen to your body's sensations, especially when you feel awe. For imagination, it's simple—make images from your inner artist, and follow the images of your life, whether through dream work or scrying or by simply walking around on the street. Signs from the Universe are everywhere, so if you pay attention and suspend your disbelief, you will tap into your intuitive intelligence. And if you're already high on logic, imagine how powerful you could become when you have both. Unstoppable.

A FEW YEARS AGO, I DECIDED TO PARTICIPATE IN AN AYAHUASCA ceremony. *Ayahuasca* is a plant medicine consumed in sacred ceremonies by indigenous peoples in the Amazon basin of South America. In recent times, this plant has become available to people all over the world, and many close friends of mine (as well as journalists and researchers) credit it with some of the most transforming and healing experiences of their lives. Now, I was expecting a transformative experience, but what I received was way beyond any expectation. It's hard to put into words, but the closest way to describe it is that I saw my babies' spirits—yes, the souls of my future children—as little shadows in the moonlight (scrying!). It was very witchy. Before this moment, I had never actually seen spirits, so you can imagine my utter shock; my inner skeptic was going bananas. I wasn't even sure I wanted to be a mother, so to meet these little gremlins was a real change in plans. The most surprising part of the experience was the infinite love and compassion I felt in my heart. There were what felt like a million star nebulas tumbling, bursting, and unfurling right in the center of my chest. And all I could do was weep (it was pretty slobbery).

In some ways, it didn't matter if what I was seeing was real. What mattered was the *feeling*—the truth I felt in my bones—that I'm meant to be a mother, whether my logical mind likes it or not. This plant helper, which shamans and healers affectionately call the mother vine, helped me unlock a deep well of maternal instinct and empathy I had long buried under the Myth of Logic. It was as I heard Tibetan monk Anam Thubten once say: "As children, we were taught everything is alive, that you can communicate with anything. We used to communicate with rats, rivers, and flowers. As we grew up, we stopped because we became more rational."

And the stakes could not be higher. Under the Myth of Logic, not only do we lose empathy for our own bodies, but we also lose the empathy needed to listen to, take care of, and mother our world. It is no wonder that the Earth's average surface temperature is getting way too high. It's no wonder that our coral reefs, known as the rain forests of the sea, are quickly roasting to death. It's no wonder our epic, structural ice caps are receding into nothing. This outer mess is a reflection of our inner mess. We've gotten far too clever and so disconnected from our own bodies—part of nature—that we've caused great suffering. We are blind to the fact that we *are* the Earth. What we do to the Earth, we do to ourselves. We are blind to the fact that we are each other. What we do to others, we do to ourselves. We have forgotten our deepest form of intelligence: love. When it comes to some of the hardest problems we're facing, such as climate change, the facts can get us only so far. We have to care in our hearts. That's why it matters that you break the spell of this myth—the tyranny of mind over body-heart-soul—so that you can give your gifts more fully, so that you can help all of us—with your *full* intelligence—clean up this mess.

Your New Toolbox

Listed here are all the tools we've explored in this chapter, along with their page numbers so you can quickly reference and practice them whenever you need to.

- Feel difficult feelings: **Mindfulness Practice** (page 141).

- Let it out: **Express Your Feelings** (page 149).

- Develop your intuition: **The Body's Yes Versus No Technique** (page 150).

- Access your inner wisdom: **The Wise Woman Within Meditation** (page 154).

- Invoke your artistry: **Name Your Inner Artist Exercise** (page 157).

- Bring your inner artist to life: **Make a Mood Board Exercise** (page 158).

- Overcome your skepticism: **Name Your Inner Skeptic Exercise** (page 160).

- Tap into your subconscious symbols and images: **Start a Dream Journal Practice** (page 163).

For further exploration and resources, including self-care rituals and meditations for the Myth of Logic, see the appendix.

7

The Myth of Harmony

The Myth of Harmony

SOUNDS LIKE

"If I just go with the flow and avoid being difficult, there won't be any problems and everyone will just get along."

LOOKS LIKE

The tendency to seek and keep harmony instead of embracing the conflict and confrontation needed for change.

MAIN STRATEGY FOR APPROVAL

Being easy to get along with, pleasant, and likable.

POWERS YOU GIVE UP

Your voice and truth.

THE MYTH OF HARMONY IS THE REASON I HAVE A TATTOO the size of my palm right above my right hip. An ex-boyfriend, F. U., was a tattoo addict, and with his encouragement I began toying with the idea of a tattoo during my last year in college. It would be sexy and mysterious and would hint at my Spanish ancestry. After casually researching options over a few weeks, we decided what the heck, let's go to the parlor to get my first tattoo together. "Whatever you do," F. U. said, "put my initials on it." Ever since we'd started dating, F. U. had had a deep-seated fear that I wouldn't love him forever. He would ask me with smoldering puppy-dog eyes, "Do you love me?" When I responded, "Yes, baby," he would follow up with "But will you love me *forever*?" Still gives me chills. Since I sensed he'd be on the verge of a breakdown if I didn't answer the way he wanted, I gave in to keep things smooth between us. "Yes, forever," I'd say, even though I didn't know if I meant it, and I was secretly praying it wasn't true.

So this tattoo would be physical proof of our "undying love." And though I didn't realize it at the time, it's clear he wanted to "mark his territory" on my body. When we arrived at the tattoo parlor, F. U. quickly abandoned me to get inked himself. That would have been my first opportunity to speak up, let him know I was nervous about getting the tattoo, and request that he stay with me. But no, I let him go.

"I have another shift in about half an hour," the tattoo artist said, holding up a piece of paper with a sketch she drew. "What do you think?" I looked down at the fan she'd drawn. To be honest, it looked kind of cartoonish, more like a shell than a fan. This moment would have been my second opportunity to speak up and let the artist know that I needed more than five minutes to think about it, and perhaps I needed to look at a few options, not just the first one she sketched quickly so she could accommodate her next shift. But alas, the Myth of Harmony was so deeply ingrained—I didn't want to be difficult or take up too much of her time. She already looked impatient. "I like it," I said. After all, we were on her schedule, and I didn't want to offend her artistic abilities.

When F. U. came back, he was euphoric and proud. "Let me see," he said, searching for his initials. He looked smug and pleased.

"Let me see yours," I said.

He turned around and peeled off one of the bandages from his bicep.

"Did you get my name or initials?"

He laughed as if it were the most absurd suggestion on the planet. "Nah, baby," he said, shaking his head. "Nah."

Even though I didn't want my name on the face of the clown he'd chosen (that really would have been fuckin' absurd), it seemed, out of principle, completely ludicrous and unfair. He was so set on showing our "undying love," but I was the only one who had to prove it with a tattoo. The implication was that he owned me, but I didn't own him. The feminist in me was dying.

I sat there fuming. F. U. definitely heard a piece from me later, but it was too late. I can't describe the horror and shame I felt afterward. I felt that at my young age, I had been damaged and claimed by this terrible man. This tattoo had sealed my fate, and I was trapped forever. I looked at myself in the mirror and imagined my pregnant body in a decade, the tattoo stretching and warping in different directions. I felt deeply scarred, ruined, and, worst of all, filled with self-loathing because I hadn't stood up for myself. I'd had choice and agency at multiple points, but I went through the motions of pleasing and agreeing, and now this—an irreversible mistake.

That day, I learned a hard lesson—stand up for yourself. When we don't speak up in the moment because we prioritize others' reactions over our own needs and desires, we make sacrifices that aren't worth it. If you're under the spell of the Myth of Harmony, you'll find that speaking up is one of the hardest things on the planet to do.

Too many of us grow up afraid of conflict, and as a result we avoid expressing anger or disappointment when we most need to. This is the central component of the Myth of Harmony. The Myth of Harmony stifles our personal growth as well as our ability to connect with ourselves and speak our truth. It holds us back in our relationships, our careers, and, collectively, in our evolution as a society. When we're under the Myth of Harmony, we're unable to see the value in social friction. Much growth can come from the tension of our differences with others. We can choose to acknowledge and work with our differences instead of bypassing and avoiding them. We need a healthy dose of friction to have authentic relationships.

When we hold back our voice, we lose so much. I see this pattern all the time in the women I work with: after years of growing up in the patriarchy, when something bothers us *we don't speak up.* For most of us, this pattern begins in our teens. Harvard University researchers Lyn Mikel Brown and Carol Gilligan found that during adolescence, girls stop speaking from their experience and expressing their true feelings and thoughts, even though they had been outspoken as children. Girls literally lose their voices, become more quiet, and say "I don't know" a million times as a way to "go underground" and hide. Why? Because, the researchers conclude, "to say what they are feeling and thinking often means to risk, in the words of many girls, losing their relationships and finding themselves powerless and all alone."[1] As one girl who was striving to be nice to others all the time confessed, "The voice that stands up for what I believe in has been buried deep inside me."[2] Brown and Gilligan realized that the irony of teen girls' strategy is that in their fear of losing connection, they refused to be honest and direct, which resulted in fake, rather than authentic, relationships.

Many of us learn the Myth of Harmony in our families. For one client, when her parents divorced, she quickly became the family's go-to peacemaker, running back and forth between her parents and negotiating their different requests. She told me, "I learned early on that conflict is really bad, that it was a sign that my family was broken and that people seemingly without conflict have better families and lives." The Myth of Harmony promises to keep us safe. It promises that if we don't speak up and say something that might upset another person, we will have better relationships. The truth is that the more we keep quiet, and therefore find ourselves off the hook in that moment, temporarily evading discomfort and fear, the longer we stay hooked into the larger problem—whether it's a situation that makes us uncomfortable or a full-blown toxic relationship.

The opposite of the Myth of Harmony is social courage. The only way to deal with the Myth of Harmony is to use our voices to break free, set and maintain clear boundaries, and lean into difficult conversations in our lives. You will no longer find yourself powerless and alone if you speak your truth. Risk it and see. You may find yourself uncomfortable, but remember, discomfort equals growth!

Speaking Up

The Myth of Harmony is a home-wrecker. Avoiding difficult conversations means you're likely to "ghost" on people when things get rocky, leaving a potentially beautiful relationship on the table and hurting the other person. Avoiding difficult conversations also means that unspoken issues fester for so long that the relationship becomes beyond repair. In its most dangerous expression, the Myth of Harmony forces you to stay in toxic relationships when you really need to leave for your own safety, well-being, and growth. Who can forget the scene in *Runaway Bride* when Richard Gere calls Julia Roberts out on her egg preferences? "You were so lost you didn't even know what kind of eggs you liked. With the priest, you wanted scrambled. With the Deadhead, it was fried. With the other guy, the bug guy, it was poached. Now, it's like, 'Oh, egg whites only, thank you very much,'" he says, referring to the multiple men she'd left at the altar. "That's called changing your mind," she argues, to which he replies, "No, it's called not having a mind of your own." Oh, snap. I have to give this one to my man Richard. When we're under the spell of the Myth of Harmony, we lose touch with that mind of our own. We go along with our partner's preferences instead of our own; we "go with the flow." We're afraid that if we oppose our partner, we'll be seen as difficult or the one to instigate fights and drama.

My friend Lara would often become swept away in her relationships, especially the early "falling in love" phase. With one boyfriend, she would party to the rhythm of her new partner, drinking beer, eating tacos, and hanging with his guy friends, and come home feeling sick to her stomach and completely exhausted. She stopped seeing her friends and doing the activities she wanted, and her self-care went completely out the window. When he had a paper to write for his MBA, she supported him by staying in his dorm for the weekend to do research and even write sections of the paper instead of going home to prepare for her own week. It was hard for her to communicate her own body's needs to her new boyfriend (because maybe he wouldn't like her anymore), to ask for time and space apart, or to set healthy boundaries that would allow both of them to properly individuate in the relationship. Some psychologists call this phenomenon codependence, and it's a fast way to poison a relationship. Broadly defined, *codependence* is when your behaviors and preferences are organized around another person, not yourself. Many clients and friends have described this as "getting sucked in," and suddenly, often by choice, supporting or living their partner's lives instead of their own. They become more passive, letting life happen to them, while their partners become more active, full of agency, will, and assertiveness. The Myth of Harmony doesn't cause codependence per se; rather, it blocks the use of our voice, which in turn can create that codependent dynamic if we're not careful.

The other way this myth plays out in our romantic relationships is that it causes us to avoid that "hard thing," a.k.a. the elephant in the room, especially if the elephant is a taboo subject like sex or money. For example, one of my clients, Jyoti, started working with me so she could get support in becoming a better leader. But as with a lot of my clients, it turned out that what she came to me for wasn't what we ended up focusing on.

Jyoti told me, "I want to start preparing for kids, but I'm nervous about how that will impact my work." I thought we were going to talk about the inevitable trade-offs women make between career and family life, but I sensed another, unspoken layer brewing beneath. "Well, plus, you know, I dread having kids," she said. "I'm not sure we can." Infertility? I wondered to myself. I could see that she was feeling shy about telling me what was truly wrong and was struggling for words. Finally, she blurted out, "We haven't had sex in a year and a half. It hurts whenever we try." She tried to normalize and dismiss it: "It's really common. So many of my friends have the same issue." Even though she and her husband had attempted and failed to engage sexually, they didn't speak about it, and so it festered below the surface of their relationship and became this "thing" that lingered between them when they tucked into bed at night. But now the issue of wanting to have kids made it impossible to ignore.

Jyoti and I worked together in sitting with the shame she felt about her situation. Having the courage to share her challenge with me was the first step. When we keep our secrets buried inside, the shame behind them only grows and festers, while bringing them into the light dissipates their power. Because Jyoti was also under the Myth of Perfection (achiever track), we worked on her prioritizing this part of her life as worthwhile to her well-being and happiness. She took a vacation day so she could visit different women's sexual health clinics, and she talked about it with her husband, who was extremely supportive.

As you can see, unspoken issues fester over time and cause problems unless you address them early on with maturity and courage. In some cases, unresolved shadows in relationships get so bad that everything crashes and burns. Returning to Lara, who was in the codependent relationship, after a few months of that unhealthy dynamic she felt miserable, like an "empty shell" of herself, and the mutual attraction she and her boyfriend had felt evaporated. Whenever she tried to exert her own voice, her boyfriend didn't respond well because it upset what had become the norm of their relationship.

Events took a very unexpected turn. Lara cheated on him as a way to press the "escape" button from the relationship. It makes no sense as a strategy, but it's more common than you may think. When we can't use our voices to stand up for ourselves throughout the relationship, or when we're too afraid to have difficult conversations and the relationship has spiraled into complete dysfunction, we find other ways to get the heck out of there. The shame Lara felt was immense, but after a good few months of therapy, she learned to forgive herself. She was able to see how she played into the dynamic and how her own good girl conditioning—the part of her that was afraid to speak her truth *throughout* the relationship—

had created a tornado that went to the point of no return. The relationship was beyond repair.

When I think about her story, what is hard for me to understand is that both Lara and her boyfriend were good people, not assholes. They were people trying to do their best, who genuinely wanted to have a healthy relationship together. But because they both embraced harmony over truth—because let's face it: he was short-term, not long-term, benefiting from her being overly harmonious—they designed a relationship that was completely out of whack. I think Lara's story shows us that it can happen to any of us and that if we are living under the Myth of Harmony, we have to be especially careful about how it may be affecting our relationships.

The Myth of Harmony works its shadow in our professional lives too. If you find yourself holding your voice back in your relationships, odds are you're probably doing the same thing at work. Even the most badass women have challenges with speaking up at work—I notice this more with creative types. In my conversation with design mogul Eileen Fisher, she confessed, "I've always been a listener, because in part, speaking was so hard for me. I've had to learn to step up and speak up more and lean into the difficult conversations; that's been a long, hard road for me. Pretty early on, I hired people to do the management and 'people work,' because it was hard for me. But now I know that there are things that matter a lot to me, and I have to speak up for those things."[3]

Jyoti shared with me that at work she had a new, younger manager, Julia, who hoped to resolve some long-standing tensions between teams and held several meetings without Jyoti. In our coaching session, Jyoti concluded that Julia must be untrustworthy, especially if she was going to exclude her from important meetings.

She planned to go over Julia's head and "casually" bring up the issue with Julia's boss during their upcoming lunch appointment.

Unlike the situation with romantic relationships, at work it can be tempting to jump to conclusions about other people's behaviors because there's less intimacy, and speaking up can feel even more risky because we can only guess how our co-workers will react. Workplaces also often breed cultures in which people relay things to other people (broken telephone style), creating gossip, fertile soil from which the Myth of Harmony *loves* to feed. When I asked Jyoti what her concern was about giving her manager direct feedback, she said, "I don't want to hurt her feelings." If Jyoti could air it out directly with her new manager, then they could potentially learn about each other and strengthen their relationship. But the Myth of Harmony prompts us to jump to conclusions and jump ship far too early, leaving a lot of potential on the table. It also prevents us from making direct requests, such as "Can I switch to this other project?" and "Can I get a raise?" because we're afraid that we'll be perceived as demanding or annoying. So, what can we do about it?

Giving Feedback

Whether it's in our romantic relationships or at work, we need to learn to speak up. Let's circle back to one of our design thinking–inspired mind-sets: *engage someone*. The best designers give courageous, honest, and thoughtful feedback because that's how the work gets better. A healthy reframe is to think about the relationships in your life as some of your most important design work. Instead of keeping your thoughts and feelings bottled up inside, the only way to improve the quality of your relationships is by continuously giving feedback. I have a term for it—*relationship hygiene*. You brush your teeth and wash your body, and it's high time you start maintaining, pruning, and scrubbing your relationships too. That way you won't build up residue underneath the surface of your relationships that leads to leaks, explosions, and funky smells that haunt you years later ("Argh, there was that time she didn't show up to my birthday party five years ago"). Yup, relationship hygiene. It's a thing. Starting now.

But if learning to give feedback to the people in your life sounds terrifying, don't worry. I have three feedback tools that will really help: the Magical Debrief, Nonviolent Communication, and Stating Your Boundaries. We'll explore each in turn.

Feedback Tool #1: The Magical Debrief

One of my favorite tools that can support you in having difficult conversations is what I call the *magical debrief*. In the world of design, every time we wrap up a project, we have a debrief—a dedicated conversation that allows for people's voices to be heard regarding what worked and what didn't. Sure, debriefing doesn't sound sexy, but it's a powerful tool to help you process, and make meaning out of, any kind of experience.

So, how do you debrief? Taking a page out of the d.school's book, here's a group or pair process that allows you to reflect (note: *not* offer criticism) on whatever happened in a way that is both constructive and useful. It's a simple process called *I like / I wish / What if* (IL/IW/WI).

"I like …"	What worked for you?
"I wish …"	What do you wish had been different? Try using "we" ("I wish we …") instead of "you" as a way to stay collaborative and avoid blame.
"What if …"	Be future-looking. Offer an idea about how to improve the situation for next time.

Here's what the d.school has to say about this process: "The IL/IW/WI method is almost too simple to write down, but it's too useful not to mention . . . Meet as a group and any person can express a 'Like,' 'Wish,' or a 'What if' succinctly as a headline. For example you might say one of the following: 'I like how we broke our team into pairs to work.' 'I wish we would have met to discuss our plan before user testing . . .' As a group, share dozens of thoughts in a session. It is useful to have one person capture the feedback (type or write each headline). Listen to the feedback; you don't need to respond at that moment. Use your judgment as a team to decide if you want to discuss certain topics that arise."[4] Pro tip: people remember negative things more than positive ones. So make sure you shower 'em with "I likes."

Obviously, this tool is typically used for giving feedback on team projects and design work, but I've found that it is effective for relationships too. Let's imagine you just got married, but you're disappointed about parts of your wedding experience, which you haven't yet aired out with your partner. Request a debrief! You can do this during a car ride, on a hike, over a meal, or in any way that feels easy. My husband and I (being more nerdy designer types) sometimes like to get intense and grab a few marker pens and sticky notes, open our laptops to take notes, and go through IL/IW/WI to surface any issues to discuss. Do what works best for you in your partnership.

Either way, this will help you surface issues that haven't gotten airtime. Surely there was much you loved about the wedding, even organizing it. And, yes, surely there was much you wish you had done differently too. The what if's help you and your partner in planning future events together, such as birthdays, holidays, or other family rituals. They help you generate solutions for family tensions and dynamics, together, as a team. Make sure to capture your debrief in writing so you can look over it years later if you need to. A dedicated debrief gives you a safe space to process what happened, use your voice to air any concerns, and set any needed boundaries for the future.

 PRACTICE THE MAGICAL DEBRIEF

Let's reflect about a recent event or collaboration with someone you love. Grab your journal or a clean sheet of paper and make three columns as shown here. At the top of the first column write "I like," at the top of the second write "I wish," and at the top of the third write "What if." Free-write your likes, wishes, and what ifs. Now, your challenge: tell that person about this process and see if they'd be open to going through it together and exchanging feedback.

I like	I wish	What if

Now, obviously the debrief is highly collaborative, and though it allows for the exchange of feedback, it isn't super targeted. For that, we need another framework, which is equally powerful and allows you to address a more specific concern with someone. It's called nonviolent communication (NVC for short).

Feedback Tool #2: Nonviolent Communication

Sandra came into our coaching session fuming at the ears. "Why didn't I say anything? I hate these people. I hate this place. How could I be so stupid?" She went on to paint me the scene.

"In the meeting, Jason was presenting about bringing publications onto the platform. At one point, he pulls up a comparison slide of 'serious' publications like the *New York Times* versus ones that aren't 'serious'—and in that column he had a bunch of Latino publications like the *Latin Times*. Everybody thought it was a hilarious joke. They all just laughed. I couldn't believe it. I just stood there and didn't say anything. I looked around, but nobody else got it. I felt so disgusted and furious."

As the only Latina in the room, Sandra had slouched in the corner with her arms crossed and lips sealed shut. This experience felt like another rude reminder that maybe she didn't belong at her company. Do you think she gave Jason feedback? No. And it wasn't her fault—the patriarchy (and a white one, at that) has trained us that a woman who speaks up is indeed a difficult (or nasty!) woman. So she kept it all bottled up inside. At our session, her fury was palpable, so I asked her to close her eyes and reimagine the moment in the meeting room after the laughter died down.

"How did you feel as you thought about saying something?"

"Really nervous."

"Let's slow down that moment. What did you feel?"

"My heart was racing and my palms were sweaty."

"Good. What else?"

"I felt a coal in my throat."

"What was this coal like?"

"Large. Burning. Almost painful."

"What were you thinking?"

"I just don't want to seem difficult. I don't want to ruin everybody's good time. Maybe I'm making a big deal out of nothing."

When we're under the spell of the Myth of Harmony, our number one fear is being judged, disliked, ostracized, rejected, hurt, or embarrassed for using our voice and exerting our will. But not speaking up does not help the situation, either, and will only hurt it in the long term. The key is to communicate what's happening for you while taking full ownership of your reactions. NVC is a four-step process developed by psychologist Marshall Rosenberg that helps us communicate feedback to others without criticism, judgment, or blame.[5] It asks us to have empathy for ourselves and others while honestly expressing our feelings, needs, and desires in a direct way—which is why I love it.

When I first discovered NVC, I was surprised by how difficult it was for me to give nonjudgmental feedback to people. I'd come off quite fierce and blame-y, pointing my finger at them, while evading any responsibility whatsoever. The Myth of Harmony forces us to be at the poles, either quiet as a mouse or swinging to the other extreme, resorting to mean and toxic strategies instead of having mature, level-headed conversations.

The revolution behind NVC is to give people feedback without judging them, which is easier said than done, trust me. Our language is typically full of judgmental words, and we're often completely unaware of how we're actually evaluating when we feel as if we're innocently telling someone what they've done wrong. People don't like to be criticized—I mean, you've been on the other end of the stick. Shitty, right? NVC offers another way.

Let's circle back to Sandra. Sandra needed to give Jason very specific feedback and set a boundary with him. Instead of letting this incident blow past her, it was time for Sandra to speak up and give her co-worker feedback in an effective and empathic way, which felt terrifying and didn't feel like "her place" but was *exactly* her place.

NVC consists of four simple steps.

1. **State the facts**—What events did you observe?

2. **State your feelings**—How did you feel?

3. **State your needs**—What is your unmet need? (Note: I like to give the option of stating values rather than needs here, which is not in the original NVC framework, if that works better in a professional context.)

4. **State your requests**—What is your request?

Sandra and I worked together to develop the following script based on NVC.

> **The fact:** "Last week during the team meeting, you presented a table with a column labeled 'serious' publications, which included the *New York Times*, and 'nonserious' publications, which included the *Latin Times*."

Notice how there's no evaluation here; rather, she's stating what was literally on the slide. If Jason were to pull up his presentation, a third-person observer would agree with the statement.

Avoid talking about words, and focus on actions. For example, if Sandra had said, "Last meeting you said Latino publications suck," her co-worker could easily counter with, "Well, no, I didn't say that," and then they'd get into a "she said/he said" argument that would have them running around in circles. So, focus on actions and observable facts. What actually happened?

The feeling: "As the only Latina in the room, I felt embarrassed and annoyed."

Okay, once the facts are down, it's time to own our feelings. Remember that Pixar movie *Inside Out*? Its genius was that it not only educated little kids about healthy emotional processing, but also, like most Pixar movies, it gave adults some tools. In the movie there are only five major feelings, all of which are characters inside the protagonist's head: (1) joy, (2) fear, (3) sadness, (4) disgust, and (5) anger. All feelings are nuances or derivatives of these five core feelings.

In this step, avoid thoughts and beliefs and focus instead on your core feelings and sensations. An example of a belief would be if Sandra shared, "I feel like you don't really care about publications from other cultures." She started the sentence with "I feel" but didn't follow it with her own feeling. Really, do your best to avoid "I feel like I" or "I feel like you," because all you will do is skirt around your true feelings. I admit, this step is the one in which you'll feel most vulnerable. It takes courage to state plainly how you feel, but it's powerful! And another thing: do your best to avoid expressing passive feelings that imply someone is doing something *to* you, such as "rejected" or "abandoned" (blame-y again!). Whenever you can't get to the bottom of a feeling, you can dig deeper by asking yourself, "And how did 'rejected' make me feel?" Keep asking until you get to a feeling that stems from one of the core five.

> **The unmet need or value:** "I value diversity and different perspectives and believe we should consider bringing publications from other cultures onto our platform, especially when they have articles on issues like immigration, college education, and Latin American politics."

Okay, we've made it this far. The next step is to state your unmet need or value and acknowledge the root of our feelings. You feel upset and triggered because one of your fundamental needs or values isn't being met. What I love about NVC is that whether you decide to use it or not, it's a helpful personal exercise to get to the bottom of your trigger. This step forces clarity on you—*what do you truly value?* But be careful: even going through this exercise can give you the illusion that you've solved the problem and it's "not such a big deal" anymore, which is a convenient way to avoid speaking up and doing the uncomfortable work of having the difficult conversation (that Myth of Harmony—so sneaky!). This step is also super important because it will help surface any differences you might have with the other person regarding underlying values and needs, and it will allow you to address those differences in an honest, open way.

> **The request:** "Can we include the *Latin Times* as a publication we'd like to bring onto our platform?"

The last step is to make a request for a specific action using clear, positive, and concrete language. Important: requests are *not* demands. Rosenberg writes, "We demonstrate that we are making a request rather than a demand by how we respond when others don't comply. If we are prepared to show an empathic understanding of what prevents someone from doing as we asked, then by my definition, we have made a request, not a demand."[6] He explains that with a request, we're open to hearing no without trying to force the matter. In other words, we respect other people's preferences and boundaries—as we would like ours to be respected, right? Instead of giving the person backlash in the form of criticism, judgment, or even guilt-tripping when they give us a no, he recommends we empathize with what's preventing the other person from saying yes before deciding how best to continue the conversation. Requests can be the hardest step for us good girls. We can find it difficult to access what we truly want moving forward and to admit it to ourselves. Often, we feel we couldn't possibly get away with making the request and fear "asking for too much." In Sandra's case, she kept telling me that her co-worker would surely laugh it off and reject her request. It's important to suspend disbelief and assumptions in this step—you don't know how the other person will react once you've taken the time to truly explain your feelings and unmet needs or values. I would say eight times out of ten, my clients come back astounded—the person was way more open than they expected, granting them their request.

What happened with Sandra? She wrote out her thoughts using NVC, and after a lot of coaching and support, she emailed them over to Jason. Though he apologized for his words being offensive and hurtful, he said he would have to think about whether to bring the *Latin Times* onto the platform and that he would discuss it with his direct supervisor. "Even though he's probably going to reject my request, I'm glad I got this off my chest," she told me.

IMPLEMENT NVC

Are you experiencing conflict or tension in one of your relationships? Maybe it's something you swept under the rug days, weeks, or months ago and now wish you had spoken up. Grab your journal and take some time to reflect to yourself first. Make a table with four rows and walk through the NVC framework—facts, feelings, needs, and requests. My challenge to you: harness your courage and put it into practice by initiating that difficult conversation you've been avoiding.

The facts	
My feelings	
My needs	
My request	

If you haven't already, I highly recommend you read Marshall Rosenberg's book *Nonviolent Communication: A Language of Life*, 3rd ed., to expand your understanding of this powerful tool.

Feedback Tool #3: Stating Your Boundaries

I have one more approach to share with you. Sometimes we need to be even more direct than when implementing NVC, especially when people are overstepping our boundaries and we don't feel safe. Let's say you live in Texas and organize a barbecue, and your brother-in-law attends with his gun tucked safely into his belt. At this point, the issue isn't social niceties; it's everyone's sense of safety. One simple tactic to think through: What are you comfortable with? What are you not comfortable with? You're comfortable with him attending and having a great time. You're *not* comfortable with him wearing his gun at your home, no matter how normal or accepted it is in Texas to do so. Before the next gathering, call him and give him a clear choice: "I'd love for you to come to our barbecue, but I'm not comfortable with you bringing your gun because it makes our family uncomfortable. I hope you will still come. We'd love to have you here." For good girls under the Myth of Harmony, this can feel terrifying because your brother-in-law might stop liking you and your sister might also get upset. But listen: if you don't speak up and set the boundary, you will be at war with yourself, anxious and worrying about how it's affecting everyone else, especially your kids. Staying quiet isn't worth it. It's time to grow up and have clear, direct conversations with people about what works for us and what doesn't.

If you start to add these feedback tools to your repertoire, I can assure you that speaking up at work and in your relationships will become easier. It doesn't happen overnight, but you are a strong, powerful woman, and with practice, it will come.

As useful as these tools are, they may not help with something deeper and more insidious, like toxic relationships. We need something a little stronger to extricate ourselves from those, so let's turn to that next.

The Bluebeard Effect

In my coaching and my personal experience, I've noticed that sometimes we don't even recognize when a relationship is toxic and stunting our growth. We don't think there's a problem (i.e., self-denial) even though our friends and family have been hinting that there might be. In other cases, we're so gripped by the fear of facing the other person's anger and disappointment that staying in the relationship allows us to conveniently avoid the difficult conversation, along with their response.

In Clarissa Pinkola Estés's iconic cult-classic book *Women Who Run with the Wolves* (a.k.a. my bible), she shares the Slavic folktale of Bluebeard. There was a man with an "eye for women" who had a beard "as blue as the shadow of a hole at night," known as Bluebeard.[7] Bluebeard was a goblin, and you knew that because his beard was an impossible bright blue that stared you right in the face. He married the youngest of three sisters, who was convinced he was not so bad ("the more she talked to herself, the less awful he seemed, and also less blue his beard"). In other words, she deluded herself into believing Bluebeard wasn't a monster, though it was probably quite obvious to everyone else around her. She symbolizes the creative potential inherent in the psyche of a woman who doesn't see herself as prey.

One day, Bluebeard went away and left his wife a key to a secret cellar but told her not to open it. Of course, she did, which is when she discovered a pile of bones and realized Bluebeard was a cold-blooded murderer. When he came back, he was furious that she had disobeyed him and wanted to murder her, but she called out for her three brothers, who slashed Bluebeard to bits. According to Estés, all these characters represent parts of a woman's psyche (even the brothers in the tale, as we can only rescue ourselves). Estés calls the Bluebeard character the "predator" part of a woman's psyche, a kind of failed magician who becomes destructive. The theory is that these outer predators we meet in our lives reflect an unresolved part of our own psyches.

When we're under the Myth of Harmony, we fall into the trap of believing that Bluebeard isn't that bad, especially in our romantic relationships. Sure, it's staring me in the face. Sure, it's super obvious to everyone else, but, but, but . . .

> *In hindsight, almost all of us have, at least once, experienced a compelling idea or semi-dazzling person crawling in through our psychic windows at night and catching us off guard. Even though they're wearing a ski mask, have a knife between their teeth, and a sack of money slung over their shoulder, we believe them when they tell us they're in the banking business.* [8]

Ahh, reminds me of the good old days with my ex-boyfriend F. U. But hey, your Bluebeard doesn't have to be your romantic partner. It can be your boss or a co-worker. One of my clients, Hannah, kept making excuses for her job, saying overly positive things like "I feel really blessed" and "I'm learning a lot," even though she was hands-down miserable. On several occasions, her boss told her that she was "too young to have a life" and made her cancel her evening plans to work after hours. Whenever she set work boundaries, her boss would be rude to her the following day, or demean her in front of co-workers, so that she set fewer and fewer of them. And listen, he was also a very charming CEO who made great promises. Like many Bluebeards, he was a very likable kind of bully, and he had an uncanny similarity to Hannah's father.

Hannah came to coaching because she wanted to quit her job, but the Myth of Harmony kept delaying her. When it was time to pull herself up by her bootstraps and quit, she would always take another look at her boss's Bluebeard—but he had taken her in, he gave her so much autonomy, and he spent many hours working alongside her—you know the drill. Hannah kept saying she was "very grateful" for her job and the opportunity, even though she was a super talented designer, a skill that was in very high demand where she lived, in Silicon Valley.

She had also been taught to "never disrespect" authorities, especially older men (Myth of Rules mentality for sure). As Estés wrote, "This early training to 'be nice' causes women to override their intuitions. In that sense, they are actually purposefully taught to submit to the predator."[9] Hannah kept ignoring the glaring evidence that this work relationship was destroying her—the fact that she was losing weight, bursting out into fits of crying, feeling out of control and completely disempowered. This job was crushing her soul.

How to Spot a Bluebeard

When in a toxic relationship, it's easy to be in a state of semidenial. We need to learn how to spot a Bluebeard. I love how Estés put it: "Our first actions must be to recognize it [the predator], protect ourselves from its devastations, and ultimately to deprive it of its murderous energy."[10]

Okay, so how do you know when someone is a bona fide Bluebeard? A Bluebeard is a person who intentionally or unintentionally sucks the living power and energy out of you. Some women feel tired, drained, dried up, brittle as if they could break at any moment, emotional with periodic breakdowns, and like they've pretty much lost their libido and passion for life. Bluebeards don't like it when you step into your power because they're very insecure. They believe if you gain too much success and power, you'll leave them behind because they're not worthy. If they see you gain too much energy, they'll do everything in their power to suck it right out of you. Your involvement with them directly opposes your growth. And under the spell of the Myth of Harmony, you'll stare lovingly at their blue beard while rocking them in your arms.

F. U. was a classic, easy-to-spot example, and perhaps you have one like him in your past or current life, but know that Bluebeards can come in all shapes, forms, and genders—they're roommates, friends, partners, co-workers, bosses, in-laws, and so forth. On the high end of the spectrum, Bluebeards could be diagnosed with a full-blown disorder like psychopathy, borderline personality disorder, or narcissism. On the lower side, however, things are a bit murkier, and we're talking about a wider pool of folks who have been traumatized and who may be well-intentioned, but because of their insecurities and unresolved wounds, are still fuckin' draining you. Some Bluebeards honestly don't *intend* to bring you down but still do. Breaking free from the Myth of Harmony is essential if you want to free up your power.

The Bluebeard Question

I've heard women tell me, "I don't think I'm with a Bluebeard, but we can't stop fighting . . ." Oh, I get it. You might hesitate to call your current boss or partner a Bluebeard . . . it feels too extreme, but you're having doubts . . . you're not sure whether it's working out. Is it worth cutting ties?

Ask yourself these two central questions.

1. Is my dynamic with this person or organization draining more energy than it's giving me? If your answer is no, then you might not have a Bluebeard on your hands, *but* you still have to wonder whether it's worth the fight. Some dynamics, for whatever reason, are just too toxic, which brings up my next central question.

2. Is my dynamic with this person sucking up so much time and energy that I'm not sharing my gifts as much as I could be? If the answer is yes, then you have a Bluebeard on your hands.

 ADMIT THE BEARD

Okay, so here you are. Let's say deep down, you can finally admit there's blue in this beard. You're ready to admit this toxic relationship is sucking up your power like one of those spooky dementors in the Harry Potter series. As they say in Alcoholics Anonymous, the first step in breaking an addiction is to admit you have one. In this case, the first step in breaking up is to stop making excuses for your job, boss, partner, parent, friend. Once you stop protecting them, what's left? Commit. Put your newfound discovery down in ink, or tell someone else. Grab your journal and write out this statement: *This relationship is a problem, and I'm done making excuses for its negative impact on my life. I'm done making rationalizations so I can avoid having an uncomfortable, scary conversation that _____ won't like very much.*

Healthy relationships are the stable ground that supports us in stepping into our power and sharing our gifts. They should not feel like earthquakes, which have you grasping for your bearings, running for cover, cleaning up the mess, and feeling floored by the time the whole thing is done. You deserve more.

Once you spot a Bluebeard, half the work is done. Next up: getting out.

Reclaiming Agency

As good girls, we've been socialized to believe we're victims and not the heroines of our own lives. This socialization can put us in a passive stance, feeling as if the world, relationships, and events are happening *to* us, robbing us of our agency and will. I've seen clients and girlfriends feel trapped, hooked, and in a loop, feeling that they have no choice, and therefore no agency to change the situation.

Trust me, I also know the feeling. I know what it feels like to fear there isn't anything better out there for me, so I might as well just go along with the program. That's what happened with F. U. and me. I was caught in a vicious cycle. One day, F. U. and I were having a rough time and fighting all day, and I decided to step out and meditate alone at my aunt's place. In my meditation, I imagined my life as a vast, luscious garden with plump fig trees, dusty, warm light cascading through the leaves, and doves splashing around in little pools of water. And then I saw it, sitting in my garden, a black vortex sucking out all the light and energy: F. U. The vision was so clear and so deep. It was my inner knowing's way of telling me, through symbolic imagery, to get out of the relationship ASAP. The meditation helped me see that F. U. was someone

I could escort out of the sacred garden. After all, he was making the doves very, very upset. Moreover, if F. U. was chilling in my garden, it was *my choice* to have him there. It was *my choice* to be in relationship with him day in and day out. There was something freeing about that notion, that I *wasn't* truly trapped. Because then it meant I could make the choice to escort him out.

The illusion of having no choice is tempting, right? In working with clients, they often tell me they're truly trapped and doomed and have no choice but to go to work or no choice but to stay in a friendship, apartment, family, or partnership. An alternative, *better* reality seems unlikely, distant, messy, and far too scary to entertain. The shitty familiar is safer than the unshitty unknown. An uncomfortable situation and relationship can be bizarrely comfortable because it's *familiar,* so we forget, amid that cozy comfort, that *we're still making a choice.* Every day, every second, we *are* making a choice, unlike many women throughout the world with less social and economic power, so let's make full use of our privilege, shall we? The first step to breaking up is taking back your agency by seeing that you have choice. Real, deep, powerful choice.*

Whenever Hannah realized she truly needed to leave her job (she would weave in and out of this awareness), she became angry at herself for not quitting sooner. Her friends were fed up with hearing her complain and urged her to get it over with already. But she stalled. And stalled. And stalled. When you know you should get out, but you don't, you experience *cognitive dissonance*—that is,

---

* If you're experiencing domestic violence or abuse or fear for your physical safety, please seek licensed professional help, as such cases are outside the scope of this book.

your actions don't align with your desires and values. Cognitive dissonance is painful, as it creates feelings of embarrassment and shame. One way to get around it is to reclaim your agency.

In one session, I guided Hannah through a visualization exercise I call the Choice Meditation to help her reclaim her agency. She closed her eyes and took a few deep breaths, getting relaxed and centered. I told her to imagine she was walking along a path that arrived at a fork. One pathway from the fork was her current situation, the default, where she was now, every day—day in and day out. I invited her to imagine what the path looked like and to get specific with details. How did the light fall on this path? Was the path grassy, muddy, or paved? Then I guided her to look down the other path. This path led to another life for herself, another possibility, something different and new. What did she feel when looking down that path? The next part of the meditation was actually the most important part—to look down at her feet and notice that she was standing at a crossroads—where she was right now. "The point is," I told her, "every day, you choose to be at this very intersection. The default pathway is actually only one among many." I could observe the deep sense of relief she felt as her shoulders melted and she let out a deep sigh. She later described this meditation as one of the most useful processes of her life. By seeing herself at a crossroads, and seeing that every day, she had

 THE CHOICE MEDITATION

If you want to reclaim your agency, practice the free Choice Meditation, which you can find on my website here: majomeditation.com.

chosen to go to work, and knowing now that she could choose differently, she could begin to take steps toward breaking free.

Use Your Voice

It's time to summon all your strength, courage, and agency to plot your escape. When it comes to a soul-sucking branch that is siphoning too many resources away from the trunk of your tree of life, you must pick up your sword and make a swift, clean cut. In Hannah's case, she was more terrified of the difficult conversation with her boss than the unknown that awaited her on the other side of quitting her job. What if he got angry? What if she disrespected or disappointed him? What if he didn't like her anymore? The prospect of using her voice to exert her desires made her fear the emotional backlash she might experience.

For a good girl under the Myth of Harmony, the step of ripping off the bandage feels the most terrifying. But it's a step we'll need to do multiple times in our lives, isn't it? Quitting the job. Leaving the program or school. Letting go of the friendship. Ending the marriage. Getting space from that family member. This step requires that fierce, courageous attitude of drawing a line in the sand with the tip of our sword, of clearing the path for our truth, creativity, freedom, meaning, and power. As Estés said, "this is the moment in which the captured woman moves from victim status to shrewd-minded, wily-eyed, sharp-eared status instead."[11]

Your voice is your most powerful sword.

Your voice isn't meant to hurt anyone, but it's meant to protect—and set a boundary for—yourself. Breaking up is never easy, but neither is growth. All growth requires pruning. After that life-changing meditation at my aunt's house, I pulled up my big-girl pants and had the heart-wrenching, beyond awkward, dramatic breakup conversation with F. U. I told him I wanted to focus on being single for a period of time and move back to the United States to figure myself out. It was hard, but guess what? The world didn't crumble. One of the best ways to make a cut is to depersonalize your reason for leaving and simply state *your desire* for the future. In my case, I could look forward to the possibilities that awaited me when I arrived back in the United States, which helped me end the relationship.

A great way to say no to one thing is to say yes to something else.

Making It Easier

What about Hannah? Even after we did the choice meditation, fear would take over again, and we'd be back to square one. Action happens when your will is greater than your fear. And though her will to leave was high, her fear was often higher. I realized that she was having dips in willpower no matter how many meditations we did, and she needed to fill up those willpower reserves some other way. I drew on the fifth design thinking–inspired mind-set— *set yourself up for success.*

When we set ourselves up for success, we remove the focus from ourselves and take a hard look at our environment. We ask ourselves one simple question: How might I change my environment to support the behavior I want? In other words, if you're running low on willpower (because fear is running high), then make the behavior very easy to do and reduce any possible barriers. So, if the action you want is *quitting*, how might you make it easier on yourself? How might you make this action, which is inherently hard, as easy as possible to do? *Setting yourself up for success* means thinking small, being realistic, and relying less on our discipline and willpower—which, if we're honest, notoriously wavers, am I right?

In Hannah's case, she was nervous about not finding the right words or screwing up in the moment, so we wrote out a script that she could practice and role-play with her friends and roommates. That made it way easier. Based on the Focus Sandwich Technique (see page 126 in the Myth of Perfection chapter), she started and ended the script on a positive note and shared her desire for the future as the filling of the sandwich. It looked like this.

- Positive: I'm grateful that I spent the last two years at this company, as I have learned so much.

- Desire: It's time that I focus on transitioning into design that focuses on financial education and services.

- Positive: Again, I want to reiterate that I've grown enormously through your guidance and I appreciate all the autonomy you've given me through the years.

Hannah was also nervous about "finding the right time," so we broke this down into smaller pieces to make it easier. The first step was putting an appointment in her boss's calendar. Next, I asked her what kind of outfit would make quitting easier for her. Even though the question sounds silly, she mentioned that if she could make herself physically taller, that would give her a boost in confidence. So we even off-loaded some of the work onto the outfit and picked out a great pair of heels for her to wear!

Another trick I learned from behavior design is social accountability—that is, raising the stakes if the behavior doesn't get done. She marked her "quitting due date" in her calendar and sent me and a few others the calendar invite. I challenged her to email five of her friends to let them know she was planning on quitting on this specific date and to make a celebratory dinner reservation for that evening. She also asked a co-worker to wait for her after her conversation with her boss and go for a walk to talk things out and offer extra support. To top it all off, because she was a champ about it, she even booked a trip to Hawaii the week after her "final week" at work, so she couldn't get sucked into some part-time or contract arrangement.

In my case with F. U., I made the breakup easier because I literally left Montreal and moved back into my parents' house in the States. Removing myself physically seemed to be the best way for me to really get out of the relationship. With physical distance, F. U. had far less power and control over me.

All this is to say, don't underestimate the power of environmental and behavioral factors to support you in getting out of your situation. Instead of relying on your discipline, willpower, or agency completely, be realistic with yourself. There's no shame in off-loading some of that work onto your environment and your support network. The following are a few more ways in which you can do that.

Behavior Design Tips

- Schedule the difficult conversation in your calendar.
- Write out a script and practice it.

- Tell friends, co-workers, and a career coach, for extra support and accountability.

- Schedule a celebration on the other side of delivering your news.

- Propose a clear end date; don't be wishy-washy.

- Physically distance yourself if needed (e.g., take a vacation right after, transfer to another team or department, stop frequenting the same spaces, move away).

- Establish a no-talk and no-see period to make the cut more clean.

Prepare for Backlash

Do you think F. U. liked it when I broke up with him? Feck no. He screamed, punched a few walls, and flailed his arms all over the place, dramatically exclaiming his life was over. Because F. U. had a giant unworthiness wound, my decision provoked it to flare up. But was that my problem? No.

You're not responsible for other people's feelings and problems. They are.

In the same way, Hannah was afraid that her boss would remind her of the big mess she'd be leaving behind and guilt her into staying. But we anticipated that response, and she began to mentally decouple herself from her company and her boss's problems—his problem wasn't her problem. The most important thing was for her to take care of herself. Anytime she felt guilty or that her boss and team really needed her, I called bullshit—she was simply afraid of the judgment she'd receive from her boss and co-workers for choosing herself first (mind you, after choosing herself second for many years). Remember, the opposite of the Myth of Harmony is social courage—the bravery to stand up for our desires and needs and set appropriate boundaries within relationships.

The greatest buffer against backlash is a support network—people who have your back and can also stand by your decision. At this point, Hannah had not only me but also five friends and a co-worker on her side, as well as her parents. Through our coaching, we had built that support network up. We recruited a stellar team. As author and culture critic Luvvie Ajayi told me during our podcast interview, "I implore women to serve as backup to each other. If you're afraid to be the first person to speak up, but you see somebody else speak up, back that person up. The more of us who use our voices, the more powerful we are, the less backlash can affect us."[12]

UP UNTIL NOW, I'VE BEEN SHARING ABOUT HOW THE MYTH OF Harmony affects *you* personally, but what about how it affects women collectively?

Once during a weeklong women's meditation retreat I attended, a group of white women became offended because a few women of color requested to pair up with other women of color for an activity. The offended group took it as an opportunity to share a lesson in spirituality with the rest of us. "Come on! I don't see race," "We're all one," and "Love is all there is, ladies!" These words sucked. They were extremely out of touch, given the long history of white women excluding women of color in feminism and the women's liberation movement (not to mention it's legitimate for people of color to create cultural sanctuaries where they can feel psychologically safe). Through convenient spiritual by-passing (you know, when you dismiss hard social realities because "we're all one"), the white women at this retreat preferred to stay comfortable and in denial of the hardships women of color endure on a daily basis.

And how many of us have done this? Too many of us want to keep things "nice" and "pleasant" and don't engage in hard conversations about inequality and justice. Of course, these are loaded, difficult, highly charged topics, but when we get to the root of it, the Myth of Harmony has trained us to pretend things are okay (maybe they are, for *us*) when they're certainly not. This avoidance and bypassing is super dangerous because that's basically how *nothing* changes and the status quo maintains its nice little front-row seat. If we want to become more empowered, we need to have hard conversations about the things that divide us as women, and as people more broadly, and about the ways we've hurt each other.

As activist and author Audre Lorde once said, "Ignoring the differences of race between women and the implications of those differences presents the most serious threat to the mobilization of women's joint power."[13] If we uphold the Myth of Harmony, any semblance of real, sustainable sisterhood—and therefore women's liberation—is doomed. We need to speak up for each other, not just ourselves. If I can leave you with one final thought about this myth, it's to think beyond yourself. Learn to use your voice, speak up, reclaim your agency, and endure the discomfort of hard conversations. *Our* freedom depends on it.

Your New Toolbox

Listed here are all the tools we've explored in this chapter, along with their page numbers so you can quickly reference and practice them whenever you need to.

- Practice sharing your preferences and desires: **The Magical Debrief** (page 183).

- Script out a difficult conversation you need to have: **Nonviolent Communication (NVC)** (page 190).

- Let others know what does and doesn't work for you: **State Your Boundaries** (page 190).

- Assess whether a relationship is toxic: **The Bluebeard Question** and **Admit the Beard** (pages 195 and 196).

- Reclaim your agency: **The Choice Meditation** (page 199).

- Make leaving a relationship or situation easier to do: **Behavior Design Tips** (preparation, scheduling, clearing deadlines, social accountability, and physical distance) (page 203).

For further exploration and resources, including self-care rituals and meditations for the Myth of Harmony, see the appendix.

8

The Myth
of Sacrifice

The Myth
of Sacrifice

SOUNDS LIKE

"I should prioritize the needs of others before my own."

LOOKS LIKE

The tendency to put other people's needs above your own at the expense of your self-care and well-being.

MAIN STRATEGY FOR APPROVAL

Being selfless, and helpful, and saving the day.

POWERS YOU GIVE UP

Your time and energy, which add up to your contribution and destiny.

THE FIRST TIME MY MOTHER SAW MY FATHER, SHE stuck her tongue out at him. "I'd like to meet that woman," my father thought. And so my parents went on their first date and fell passionately in love. My mother, a bad-ass with a sexy overbite and wild, poofy hair, was a well-known anchorwoman on a local news channel in her hometown of Rosario, Argentina, paying her own way through law school in the early 1980s. Her independent, fiery intensity could be matched only by a man like my father, a medical student who wore a leather jacket and rode a motorcycle (I know, exactly like Che Guevara).

When my father was accepted into medical residency in the country's capital, Buenos Aires, my mother picked up her life and left with him. She quit her television job and fought hard to transfer her credits to the prestigious law school at the University of Buenos Aires. "It was my first culture shock of many," she told me. "I left my family behind and married a man I'd dated for only a few months. It was risky." Argentina was a political and economic mess at the time, so when my dad landed a postdoctoral fellowship at the University of Toronto Faculty of Medicine, they didn't think twice, and my mom, now with two little kids under the age of three, followed him the week after she graduated.

"Even though I studied hard for eight years," my mother told me, "I haven't practiced law a day of my life. I don't think I fully understood what I was giving up. I was kind of blind." Without a work permit, my mom worked under the table as a hostess at a hotel in Toronto. When they offered to promote her to the night shift, my father resisted. "You can do better," he told her. But because of the culture shock and language barrier, my mom didn't feel she could. She ended up continuing her work at hotels, malls, department stores, and jewelry shops, not because she needed to (my father's salary covered us) but because she wanted to preserve her identity outside her role as mother and wife. "Any work is dignified," she would tell me. "Even picking up the phone."

Growing up, it was heartbreaking to see my mother, who was such a talented woman, sacrifice her career, potential, and gifts for our family. "Do you think Dad would have done it for you?" I asked. "No way," she replied.

Sacrifice is a core part of the immigrant narrative. A generation sacrifices itself for the next one so more opportunities can continue down the line. Sacrifice is the very reason I'm here writing this book. If my parents had not decided to leave their home country, I wouldn't have the incredible opportunities I have today. When it's motivated by choice and love, sacrifice is wonderful. A mother gives up her life for her child. A firefighter sacrifices his safety to protect us from raging fires—acts that are undoubtedly heroic. The problem is when, for thousands of years and across thousands of cultures, the burden of sacrifice falls more heavily on the backs of women. When I look at our family's immigration story, I see it was my mother who sacrificed the most to keep our family together. As she would tell me years later, "In my tradition and culture, in the name of love and family, a woman abandons her career to support her man. You simply follow."

My mom is certainly not alone. Under the Myth of Sacrifice, we leave behind our homes, our families, and our sense of history, identity, and place for others. We give up our visions for the future—our careers, passions, interests, and gifts—because of our trained sense of duty and responsibility in our roles as mothers, partners, sisters, daughters, and friends. While some of us, like my mother, default into a supporting role and others consciously choose it (for example, a woman who decides to leave work to focus on motherhood), *all* of us—since we were little girls—have been bombarded by examples of women fully inhabiting their relationship duties, often at the expense of their own well-being. *This* myth is the most contagious of all myths, one that cascades effortlessly like a waterfall down multiple generations.

If it isn't our duty as mother, it's our duty as daughter and spouse that consumes us. In many cultures, women take on the brunt of the caregiver burden through traditional notions such as filial responsibility (caring for one's elders) and familism (prioritizing family needs over individual ones). Studies show that women, especially those sixty-five years of age and older, provide care for elders for a longer period of time and for more time per day than men, and they report higher levels of depressive and anxious symptoms and lower levels of physical health and overall life satisfaction.[1] According to a research summary by Professor Darby Morhardt at the Alzheimer's disease center at the Northwestern University Feinberg School of Medicine, women "express a greater sense of responsibility towards family members, altruism, and self-sacrifice" than men.[2] Traditional gender roles ask that women care for others, which the patriarchy perfectly reinforces when women are paid less than men for exactly the same work outside of the home.

The point is that sacrifice in the name of family duty is what we've experienced and learned for centuries. Today, while we can feel like strong, independent women, the Myth of Sacrifice still runs in the background (remember, thousands of years of conditioning), encouraging the kind of helper mentality that is at the core of caregiving: we overextend ourselves for others, without even realizing it, in a way that sabotages us in the long run.

"I don't realize I'm doing it, which means it's my biggest energy leak," one entrepreneur told me. I hate to say it, but many of us are still subconsciously fulfilling this gender norm. I've had clients volunteer to help without being asked, or say yes to helping because they felt obligated, internalizing other people's problems. The guilt of not helping is too much. But we don't realize that by helping, "just this one time," we are actually *sacrificing* the time and energy we could be using to do our deepest work and to prioritize our mental and physical health so that we can give our gifts. Unconscious helping behaviors are a slippery slope down to the Myth of Sacrifice, because our destiny is the sum of our small daily choices.

When we sacrifice without realizing we are, we drink poison in the form of bitterness, anger, and resentment that can stay with us for days, months, and years, as it did for my mother. "It was obviously my choice," she would later tell me. "But I *thought* I wanted it. I look back and wonder, gosh, why did I do that? I wouldn't do that today. I'm angry at myself for all the potential I left behind."

It's time to snap ourselves out of this myth and do the work to reclaim our lives. When we overcome the Myth of Sacrifice together, we create a world where women aren't sacrificing their dreams or tied up in caregiving (again, unless they want to be) but are using their genius and brilliance to cocreate the future, find solutions to pressing problems, contribute their ideas, unleash their creativity, and ultimately shape history with their voices. The task is big, but the steps are small. In this chapter, we're going to learn how to reclaim our time by prioritizing self-care and how to reclaim our energy by setting up solid emotional boundaries.

Reclaiming Time

One of the first boundaries we need to set is around time. We often hear that time is money. But time is far more than money. Time is life. Time is attention. Time is energy. Time is choice. Time is power. Time is freedom. Freedom to be, create, and lead. Time is a precious resource—and it's one of the first we learn to sacrifice for others as good girls.

Here are some ways we sacrifice our time for others.

1. We schedule activities that support another person's goals or dreams instead of our own.

2. We prioritize our duties as part of our family and caregiving roles to the extent that we forget what we want and need.

3. We automatically say yes to helping others because we feel responsible for their problems and feel bad if we don't help out.

4. We (and our calendars) are readily available and open to others whenever they need us.

At the core, it's a sense of obligation and duty that leads us to give our time away so freely. My client Steph, a twenty-nine-year-old artist from Maine, had moved back home with her parents after quitting her job so that she could save money and bootstrap her new ceramics business. Even though she had all the time in the world, she hadn't focused on her business or craft. Instead, she found herself wrapped up in household chores, which was fine for a period of time, but after three months of making zero progress on her dreams, I became concerned.

"I just feel bad when I don't help," Steph told me during a coaching session.

"Let's go into that feeling," I said. "Tell me more about 'feeling bad.'"

"If I don't help around the house, I'm a bad daughter."

"Keep going. What else are you?"

"I'm selfish."

"What else?"

"I'm spoiled. Taking advantage of my parents."

"Is that what you are when you get behind your wheel to make your bowls? Bad, selfish, spoiled?"

"Yes. My art feels selfish, especially when my parents work."

"What do you do when you feel that you are selfish?"

"I try to get rid of the feeling."

"How?"

"By being a good daughter."

"What makes you a good daughter?"

"Doing what my parents need from me, such as chores around the house."

As you can see, even though Steph consciously wanted to spend time on her business, the Myth of Sacrifice was running the show behind the scenes. There's no doubt that she should help her parents, but the main purpose of her leap was to focus on jump-starting her business. If you believe your desires and needs are selfish and you're a "bad fill-in-the-role" for pursuing them, of course you will avoid them. Is it selfish to make beautiful, meaningful art? No, even if it is a privilege.

Reactive Versus Responsive Time Orientation

Through the years, I've observed two kinds of time orientations: reactive and responsive.

Reactive

A reactive time orientation happens when we react to other people's needs and desires. When we have this time orientation, people can schedule meetings into our calendar whenever it pleases them. We reflexively say yes to requests without truly seeing whether they line up with our greater vision or deeper *why*, all because we want to be helpful or we feel responsible for other people's problems. A reactive time orientation is about picking up the phone at random times during the day, whenever it rings, whenever you receive a text. It's about having the door to your office wide open, so anyone can walk in and distract you with conversation or requests. It's about volunteering your time because you're being reactive to another's discomfort (or your own uncomfortable emotions of guilt and obligation). A reactive time orientation means putting others first and yourself second. In a reactive orientation, your time is depleted until there's barely any left for you. If you're under the spell of the Myth of Sacrifice, odds are you're living from this kind of time orientation.

Responsive

In a responsive time orientation, on the other hand, we consider every request, opportunity, and commitment with intentional pause. Here are the questions we might ask ourselves.

- Does this engagement feel like a yes or a no in my body?
- Does this engagement line up with my needs, desires, or goals?
- What is my intention for saying yes (a sense of obligation or genuine desire) or no (a focus on other priorities)?
- What are my existing commitments?

A responsive time orientation is about creating space between someone's request and your response. Instead of defaulting to yes, say, "Let me get back to you." It's about having time boundaries.

It sounds basic, but the easiest way to shift from a reactive to a responsive time orientation is to plan your time. Steph's calendar, for example, was far too open and unstructured after she moved back home, making her susceptible to getting off track. *Every* woman—whether she's a stay-at-home mom, retiree, recent graduate, or career woman—must plan her calendar, or else her time will become other people's time. I can't tell you how many of my clients don't fill out their calendars with *what supports them first* and then end up getting swept into other people's agendas and timelines. Planning your time, which is vital to experiencing it with more freedom and ease, will support you in staying responsive.

The first step is to have a calendar you regularly design and maintain (no, you don't simply "set it and forget it"). Your calendar doesn't need to be fancy or formal, but it does need to give you a solid sense of your daily and weekly rituals and how they work toward your deeper goals and values, as well as how you want to feel and who you want to be in this phase of your life. When we don't write down our commitments, they churn around in our minds instead, draining our mental energy. Capturing and externalizing them is vital to creating more mental space for ourselves.

For Steph, she needed to mark her own time first and then find windows of time to support her parents. That way, when her mother asks her to launder the sheets, she doesn't drop what she's doing or rush to get it done right away (reactive time orientation) but considers her goals for the day first (responsive time orientation). There would be times in her calendar that are nonnegotiable "Steph" time. She would certainly get to the laundry, but she'd plan for it to happen later in the evening or on the following day during her designated "chores" time, which is something she could discuss and negotiate with her parents. What do we, as women, need to block out in our calendars above all else? That's where we're going next.

Protecting Your Self-Care

Self-care isn't something we "have to do" but a natural extension of caring about ourselves. When we feel we're worthy and love ourselves, we take care of ourselves. Self-care isn't about fixing, shaming, or correcting ourselves (like going on an intense diet) but about genuinely wanting to be healthy, well, and whole.

Why do we need it? For one, we're way more effective in giving when we take care of ourselves first. We have more energy and stamina and a generally positive mental attitude. We're giving from a centered place, instead of a frantic or exhausted one that might lead us toward making mistakes and experiencing more bitterness. The effects are cascading, and it starts with self. Self-care is the inner work that allows us to be more effective in our work in the world. Period.

When I asked Steph about her self-care, I learned we had different definitions.

"Watching a show with my folks," she said. "Or getting ready with my friends and going out to a bar. Things that are fun."

"What do you notice about how your body feels after watching a show or going out?"

"My body? Nothing, sometimes a bit tired. I mean, if I go out, the next day I feel hungover."

"Why do you consider these activities self-care?"

"I guess 'cause I'm getting my mind off work."

True self-care includes all the activities that *nourish* your mind, body, and soul. But like Steph, too many of us confuse activities that numb us with those that truly nourish us. Binge-watching a new show may be pleasurable and feel like you're treating yourself after a long day of work, but do you feel more refreshed and energized? Activities that give us a shot of pleasure in the short term often don't give us the deeper, more sustainable energy we need to feel both rested and energized (the true yogi state of mind, by the way).

Obviously, activities like watching TV aren't *all* bad, *all* the time, but they can't replace what's truly nourishing. I don't blame Steph for equating self-care with things that are fun. We live in a world that stimulates and bombards our senses, selling us so-called entertainment and leisure as self-care. Pop culture (and capitalism) teach us to equate relaxing, taking a vacation, and letting go with going to Las Vegas and overstimulating ourselves with the bright slot machines and loud club music. I had a meditation teacher who used to remark that people typically come back tired and undernourished from their extravagant getaways. When we're truly honest with ourselves, it's clear that those experiences don't actually give us energy. On the contrary, they deplete us or make us crave more stimulation, which in turn pulls us into an addictive loop. We become desensitized and need more and more to feel good, or to feel anything at all.

It isn't self-care when we leave feeling like we "had a good time" while our bodies are ultimately beat up and worn down. Self-care is also *not* about avoiding the hard realities of your financial situation, for example, by getting tipsy with a glass of wine and passing out in the evenings. It's *not* about soaking in a tub to avoid the difficult conversation you have to have with your spouse about your rocky marriage (Myth of Harmony, anyone?). Self-care is about cleaning up those larger issues like an adult, as well as making space and time to nourish your mind and body.

As we work to include more self-care in our lives, let's apply one of our mind-sets inspired by design thinking: *make something*. As we learned with the Myth of Perfection, prototypes are small versions of our ideas and goals that we can create and test right away (as opposed to delay and procrastinate). Prototypes aren't always physical; they can also be experiential. In a sense, we can

UNDERSTAND YOUR SELF-CARE

Take some time to reflect on the following questions and write your responses down in your journal.

- What are some activities I engage in that feel good in the moment but actually help me numb and distract myself?
- What are some activities that feel deeply nourishing?
- What does nourishing feel like in my body? What about numbing?

prototype *anything*, especially our actions. So let's create and test our self-care rituals out in the wild. In my experience of doing self-care rituals for years, and supporting women in designing their own, I've noticed they help us feel more grounded and less fragmented, especially in a world that's groping for our attention twenty-four seven. It's one of the most powerful forms of boundaries we can have. How is it different from a routine? This is an important question; let's take a look.

Self-Care Ritual	Routine
Intentional	Automatic
Mindful activities	Habitual activities
We make choices	No choices needed
No interruptions allowed	Interruptions allowed
Solitude	Other people allowed

Self-Care Ritual	Routine
Being present through the senses	Moving on to the next thing
Focus on beauty, sensuality, and pleasure	Focus on function
Nourishes us	Gets the job done
No work, productivity, or distractions	Work, productivity, and distractions allowed
Solid boundaries needed	Boundaries not necessarily needed
Closed container with a beginning and end	Open container that leaks into the day

As you can see, a routine is mostly functional (e.g., brush teeth) and automatic, something that allows us to get on with our day and may not include boundaries with regard to other people and distractions. Because so many of us wake up in the morning anxious and overwhelmed by our responsibilities and to-do lists, we typically run through routines (not rituals), missing opportunities for self-care. As a highly creative achiever type (with a moon and rising in Virgo), I will confess that I *love* routines. The beauty of mindless habits is that we don't have to make a million decisions before we head into deeper, more creative work. If you study the lives of great artists, you'll realize that many of them had extremely rote (and quite uncreative) routines.[3] That said, you can combine the best of both these approaches to design a self-care ritual that works for you. How? By weaving nourishment and beauty into your existing routine in small and accessible ways. You don't have to start from scratch or move to an ashram, I promise. I want to invite you to become your own ritual designer, using the powerful principles of behavior design to meet yourself *exactly* where you are.

How to Design Your Self-Care Ritual

1. Capture Your Routine

Let's begin where you are. Write out the way you currently move through your morning or evening. There might not be a set order to the events, but what are the actions you're already taking? It's okay if your current routine has a lot of variety in it and if you don't do every action every day—a rough list is fine.

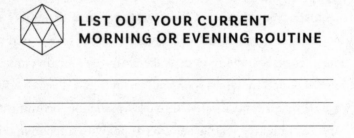

LIST OUT YOUR CURRENT MORNING OR EVENING ROUTINE

_____

_____

_____

Here's what Steph generally did every morning.

Example: Steph's Routine

1. Feed dog
2. Toilet/wash face
3. Walk dog
4. Shower

5. Cook breakfast
6. Eat breakfast
7. Get dressed

2. Choose One to Three
New Self-Care Activities

List out three new self-care activities. My recommendation is to choose an activity that falls into one of the four following categories: food and water, sleep, exercise and movement, or mental rest and clearing. For Steph, we determined she wanted to weave yoga and journaling into her mornings. Don't add more than three new self-care activities at a time. In fact, the best approach is to add one, and once that's down for a few days, add the others. Research shows we have a limited amount of discipline, and when we try to form too many new habits at once, we have trouble holding them down.[4]

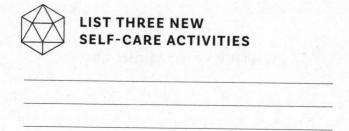

**LIST THREE NEW
SELF-CARE ACTIVITIES**

_____

_____

_____

3. Identify Possible Anchors
from Your Current Routine

We know Steph's current routine and what she wants to weave in. The best move is to piggyback her new behaviors onto what she's already doing. She can do this by leveraging what Stanford's behavior scientist, professor, and author BJ Fogg calls _anchors_. What's an anchor? According to Dr. Fogg, anchors help people develop tiny habits because they're existing, solid behaviors that you can attach your new behavior to.[5] An anchor is a behavior you do without fail, every day. Anchors can be very small and automatic, like raising the blinds in the morning or getting out of bed. They tend to cluster around bed and bathroom activities, which happen at both the beginning and end of our day. Many anchors depend on our environment, but the best ones would exist regardless of where we are. Imagine you're in a hotel in Prague. What would you still do without fail? Put in your contacts? For most of us, the best anchor is brushing our teeth, but there are many others, more than you think (e.g., using the restroom, putting the kettle on the stove, grabbing your car keys). Dr. Fogg advises that you put your new behavior right *after* your anchor. He even recommends you make a clear "After I . . ." statement, such as "After I turn off the light, I will exercise for five minutes."

 IDENTIFY YOUR ANCHORS

Return to your routine in Step 1 and circle at least one possible anchor. Rewrite your routine, adding one of your self-care rituals after your anchor (see Steph's example on the next page for reference).

For Steph, we narrowed down to two possible anchors: washing her face and cleaning up after breakfast. Because we weren't sure which one would be best, we decided to keep it open and test out both. It's okay to identify more than one anchor, though best to test one at a time. Once you put it into practice, it will become clear which one is the best one for you right now. We wrote out her sample schedule as such.

Example: Steph's Ritual

1. Feed dog

2. Toilet/wash face —
   Anchor Option 1

3. Yoga and journaling —
   Possible Location 1

4. Walk dog

5. Shower

6. Cook breakfast

7. Eat breakfast/clean up —
   Anchor Option 2

8. Yoga and journaling —
   Possible Location 2

9. Get dressed

4. Identify Possible Bookends from Your Current Routine

Your self-care ritual must have an opening and an ending. It's a "container" with boundaries. When I started doing ritual practice, I noticed a challenge—I'd get distracted (often by my phone or cleaning around the house), time would go by, and I wouldn't make it to the end to close the loop. I would suddenly feel rushed to get ready for my day. Knowing my bookends helped. Once I open my book, my intention is to honor and close it. A bookend is a micro-action that you will open and close your ritual on. If my first action is taking a shower, I begin my ritual by turning on the knob (opening bookend). If my last action is eating breakfast, I end my ritual by cleaning my dishes (closing bookend). These micro-actions serve as mental cues that I'm opening and closing the ritual. Extra points to you if you take a deep breath during your bookends, infusing your ritual with more intention. If you can't think of a natural bookend, light a candle, keep it on until you close your ritual, and blow it out. It's small and simple, and the sight of the candle burning will remind you that your ritual is still happening.

For Steph, we decided that her opening bookend would be making her bed in the morning and her closing bookend would be brushing her hair, which would signal to her that the ritual is over and she's ready for her day.

What's nice about bookends is that whether you decide to have a luxurious two-hour morning ritual or a quick twenty-minute one, your bookends can remain the same and will keep you focused. Think of your ritual as an accordion that you can stretch or shorten depending on your bandwidth, energy, and time. With rituals, you want to strike that balance between structure and flexibility. If you're too rigid, you'll feel like a robot and get bored or feel the tyranny of your own rules! If you're too flexible, you'll get decision fatigue or not do your rituals at all. Bookends will help you feel fluid and focused.

 IDENTIFY YOUR BOOKENDS

Take your new list from Step 3 (the one with your anchors and new activities) and add in your opening and closing bookends (see Steph's example below for reference).

Example: Steph's Ritual

1. Make bed —
   Opening Bookend

2. Feed dog

3. Toilet/wash face

4. *Yoga and journaling (test)*

5. Walk dog

6. Shower

7. Cook breakfast

8. Eat breakfast

9. *Yoga and journaling (test)*

10. Get dressed

11. Brush hair —
    Closing Bookend

5. Test and Adjust Your New Ritual

Whenever I talk to clients like Steph about designing their ritual, it's all very hypothetical. We imagine what might be possible, but we don't really know until they try it out in their environment. That's why we have to have a testing and adjustment period. Things come up in your environment (and also in interactions with partners, pets, kids, etc.) and opportunities you hadn't seen before arise. It's best to test run your ritual for a week and make updates. Jot down a few observations in your journal about what you're learning.

Steph came back. "Okay," she said. "I tried both ways, before and after, and you know, I've got to say, it was easier afterward. The guilt wasn't gnawing at me, and I could focus more. So after breakfast, before getting dressed, I went back into my room and did some yoga and journaling. It worked."

Example: Steph's Ritual

1. *Bookend:* Make bed

2. Feed dog

3. Toilet/wash face

4. Walk dog

5. Shower

6. Cook breakfast

7. Eat breakfast — **Successful Anchor**

8. Yoga and journaling — **Successful Location**

9. Get dressed

10. *Bookend:* Brush hair

Another way you can *set yourself up for success* is by shaping your environment to support your new rituals. You can design your environment to help you make your ritual feel more effortless and in flow. Here are a few tips for how to do so.

Tip #1: Redesign Based on Space

Space is as important as time. Every behavior you do happens within a space and involves a set of objects. When we first designed Steph's ritual, we didn't make any major changes to her flow because I wanted to test her simply inserting a new activity. But if you want to take your ritual design a step further, I recommend redesigning it based on space. The idea of redesigning based on space isn't to become more efficient, necessarily, but to make behaviors feel like they flow and are easier for you to do. When a behavior is easier for you to do, you will be more likely to do it. It will also minimize distractions, as you won't be traversing long distances and looking at a bunch of objects along your way. As you can see below, Steph's ritual was spatially spread out all over the house, causing her to run back and forth between different rooms.

Room/Space	Activity
Bookend	Make bed
Kitchen	Feed dog
Bathroom	Toilet/wash face
Outside	Walk dog
Bathroom	Shower
Kitchen	Cook and eat breakfast
Bedroom	Yoga and journaling
Bedroom	Get dressed
Bookend	Brush hair

DO YOUR NEW SELF-CARE RITUAL

There's nothing like actually doing your ritual to know how it feels and whether it works. Look at your calendar and choose one of your more spacious upcoming mornings to try this ritual. Put it in there. Extra bonus points if you send a calendar invite to someone else to be your accountability buddy.

Do you see any opportunities to rearrange your rituals based on space? You can make several versions and possibilities of the morning ritual quickly. When we visualize something, it allows us to consider new possibilities we hadn't seen before when we were thinking linearly. As part of visualizing, ask the question "What if X were like Y?" It's all about flipping our perspective and discovering new ways of seeing a problem. Let's try it.

VERSION 1

What if Steph's ritual were like a concentric circle? We grouped and sequenced activities together that happened in the same space and visualized the bathroom being the most intimate, internal room in the center, with the spaces getting progressively more external until she walks the dog.

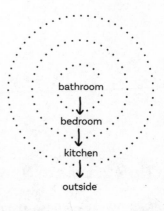

Keep in mind that when you rearrange your ritual based on space, you may need to readjust your anchors and bookends. Opening bookends tend to be fixed, as they relate to waking up, which everyone does, while closing bookends typically need adjustments. In this version, her new anchor became getting dressed instead of eating breakfast, and her closing bookend became hanging up the dog's leash.

VERSION 2

What if her ritual were more like a sandwich? We could place more internal activities, like those in the bathroom and bedroom (which were conveniently adjacent), at the ends and her responsibilities (which involved more communal and external spaces) at the center. This version would potentially support Steph in transitioning into her studio work more easily. She would take care of herself first, shift to her family duties and chores, and then take care of herself at the end again.

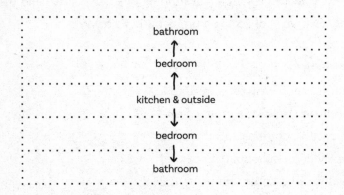

Tip #2: Create New Space

New behaviors also require new space. For reflective and contemplative exercises, I encourage my clients to create an altar or contemplative nook for themselves in their home, ideally in their bedroom or an adjacent room.

**HOW TO CREATE AN ALTAR OR DEDICATED
SPACE FOR CONTEMPLATIVE RITUALS**

1. Choose a corner or place against a wall.

2. Get a small table (even a crate you flip over and cover
   with a shawl).

3. Put objects of significance on it, like a plant, a candle,
   or photos of family.

4. Find comfortable seating, such as a shag rug or cushion.

If you want to do more exercise, can you create an exercise
area? Roll out a mat, or find easy access to a gym or a slice of grass
outside. Choose a dedicated space for whatever new behaviors you
want to create.

Tip #3: Create Visual Cues and Hide Distracting Objects

Our rituals involve objects too. Though I'm all for minimalism, I
actually believe putting objects out into the open where you can
see them is better for your self-care rituals. These objects then
trigger and remind you to start or stay with your ritual. Steph
placed her journal right on her night table and kept her yoga mat
rolled in the corner (and sometimes rolled out), making it easier
to flow with her ritual. When she woke up, her eyes caught these
objects, reminding her that she needed to come back to her room
to complete her ritual. This is another benefit to creating an altar
or dedicated nook to do a ritual.

On the flip side, some objects will distract you from finishing
your ritual. A really comfy-looking unmade bed will certainly invite
you back in for more sleep. Last night's open chocolate bar on the

counter will invite you to eat it instead of cooking a nourishing breakfast. And by far the most distracting object you can have is your phone. Don't use your phone as an alarm, and charge your phone outside of your bedroom. Turn your phone off at night, and turn it on in the morning after your ritual. Your phone is a gateway to a world of social interactions and information that will take, take, take from your self-care time if you don't have solid boundaries.

If you go through these steps, you will have a solid self-care ritual designed. Remember, think like a designer. Design, test, and adjust the ritual as you see fit. Your ritual is a living, breathing practice you actively shape.

Reclaiming Energy

Now that we've covered prioritizing ourselves by designing self-care rituals, let's talk about reclaiming our energy. Another way we get hooked into the Myth of Sacrifice is by not having emotional boundaries.

Take my client Greta, a thirty-four-year-old executive assistant, who had spent the past four years in recovery from an eating disorder and recently landed her first major job in the fashion industry. During one of our coaching sessions, she tried to make sense of a former lover's unexpected reappearance in her life.

"He drove eight hours to see me," she said. "I'm disappointed in myself."

"Why?"

"Because I told myself I wouldn't sleep with him, but I couldn't hold my ground."

"What shifted for you?"

"He's in recovery, you know. I know what it feels like to be doing your best to get better. He crawled into my bed on the verge of crying, helpless. I felt for him."

She crossed and uncrossed her arms and picked at the cuticles on her fingernails. Underneath Greta's perpetual nervousness was a sweet, genuinely caring smile—a desire to connect, to love and be loved. Greta is what I'd consider a highly sensitive, emotionally empathic woman. When she watches a movie and the protagonist cries, she cries. When a friend is feeling low, she feels low with them. When a random stranger screams at her on the subway, she absorbs their anger. In other words, she feels a lot. Emotional empaths experience "emotional contagion," which is when other people's emotions feel particularly contagious to them and they get hooked into them. Many of us good girls are emotional empaths. As an emotional empath myself, I can walk away from a conversation and suddenly feel enormously tired and cranky, when I'd been fine a few minutes earlier. If I'm not careful, I catch other people's "emotional bugs." We empaths need to learn healthy emotional boundaries in order to reclaim our energy.

What Are Emotional Boundaries?

An *emotional boundary* is what it sounds like—a boundary between another person's emotions and our own. Emotional boundaries protect our hearts, minds, and souls and allow us to stay with our own truth and self-authority. They create a healthy distance between ourselves and other people. This distance gives both parties their own ability to be themselves as intact, empowered individuals. Emotional boundaries are about not hooking into other people's emotions and problems but letting them pass through you and eventually letting them go altogether.

Let's say your friend comes to you feeling devastated because her girlfriend broke up with her for the third time. She laments to you about how her girlfriend is a selfish and uncaring woman. You soothe her cries and let her express her pain and anger. While she's complaining, you deeply empathize with her suffering; she feels abandoned yet again. You can see that your friend is hurt and triggered, that she isn't getting what she wants or needs from her relationship.

You care, enough to listen with full attention, but because of your emotional boundaries, you're not going to absorb or internalize her negative feelings. You're not going to leave the conversation feeling angry, hurt, and abandoned yourself. You're not going to call your friend's girlfriend up and tell her off. Instead, you're going to be fully present for her and move on. You may check in on her with some sweet texts or send her some flowers. But her life isn't your life. Her problems aren't your problems. Her feelings aren't your feelings. Emotional boundaries keep us from getting reactive, which usually involves trying to help or save someone else, which is a bit arrogant because it assumes we know better than they do.

When we don't have emotional boundaries, we feel drained and overwhelmed. As an executive assistant, Greta found herself "holding space" (being the shoulder to cry on) for her boss, who had recently lost her nephew in a car accident.

"She unloads on me. And I just listen."

"How does it feel?"

"I actually like it, because it makes us feel closer. But then I can't get my admin tasks done for her that day because I'm overwhelmed. Tired. Scattered."

On top of all these energy-consuming relationships, Greta was beating herself up for not dedicating more time to her service project—fund-raising for a homeless shelter in Detroit. "The guilt about it kills me," she said. "I try to follow through on commitments with the nonprofit, but I'm stretched thin. And scared of relapsing."

Though Greta needed to focus on her own healing journey, she felt responsible for everybody else's problems, whether at work or beyond. Greta, like many of us, needs some emotional boundaries so she can parse what's hers and what's somebody else's.

Read carefully: it's possible to be fully empathic and have emotional boundaries. As good girls, we earnestly want to be good friends, good mothers, good partners, good employees, and the list goes on. Some of us fear that if we have emotional boundaries we can't be good friends. A woman once asked me, "How do I balance being a good friend with having emotional boundaries? Sometimes my friend is having a hard time and wants my support, but I'm just not up for it. How do I deal with the guilt? I want to be responsive to the people I love but don't want to absorb their negative stuff."

This woman hadn't yet learned how to engage with her friend (and her friend's problems) while maintaining emotional boundaries. As a result, she found it easier to keep physical distance and avoid interaction. This is a common way to cope, but we risk not being honest with our friends about why we're pulling away. We need to strengthen our emotional boundaries (I'll get into how shortly) so that we can show up for the people we love. When we have emotional boundaries, we actually become *better* in our relationships.

An important caveat: some folks thrive off your *not* having emotional boundaries. These are people who want you to agree with and play into their dysfunctional stories and beliefs about themselves and the world. When you don't, they get offended or mad. In my younger years, I had a short-lived friendship with a woman who would ask me leading questions: "Don't I look fat in these jeans? Don't you agree that he was an asshole? Don't you think I should speak up about this?" And I would simply ask, "Do you? What do you think?" Or I would be honest and tell her what I truly thought: "No, he's definitely not being an asshole." Her questions annoyed me, and my answers annoyed her (perfect!), so we stopped being friends (refer to the Myth of Harmony about toxic relationships). Unless you or the other person is being an energy vampire, having emotional boundaries should improve, not hurt, your relationship.

How to Have Emotional Boundaries

Okay, so let's get to it. How do we create emotional boundaries? First, recognize when you most need them. We need emotional boundaries *in the moments* we're confronted with other people's problems and negative emotions, such as complaints, rants, gossip, and sticky, difficult emotions like anger, shame, guilt, disgust, and fear, especially when they're wrapped up in dysfunctional stories.

Second, practice mindfulness. The most effective way to create and maintain an emotional boundary is to bring your attention from the other to yourself. Have you ever noticed that when someone is going on and on about their problems, you can feel like you're falling into them? We get absorbed, in the same way we might be absorbed by the heroine's tragedy in a movie and find ourselves crying, as if we ourselves were the heroine. That's because great

stories and drama hook our attention. The key is to not lose ourselves in other people and to become aware of our own bodies. Do
this experiment right now: Drop your attention down to your feet,
specifically the soles of your feet. Feel them make contact with
the ground. Bring your attention to your feet and notice how that
subtly shifts your experience of reading. You feel a bit more embodied, right? When you bring your attention to your feet, you're
concentrating more energy in them, which is a grounding action,
since your feet connect you to the Earth. Feeling grounded in our
bodies is important because it helps us feel more emotionally and
mentally centered instead of scattered. When we're worrying or
thinking about the past or the future, we're not grounded in our
bodies. When we're grounded in our bodies, we're in the present moment, which is where life is happening. When someone's
talking to us, our energy is typically either diffused or hooked into
them. When you bring your attention to your feet, however, you're
containing your energy. Try it next time someone is going off on
you. It's a simple but powerful technique. You will walk away
feeling less swayed by the other person's emotions.

Another powerful (and free) ally is your breath. If someone
is going off on me, I'll loosen up my belly and take a few deep
breaths. This also brings my attention (therefore energy) farther
down my body and helps me contain my energy. And if you want
bonus points, try bringing your attention to both your breath and
feet at the same time. It's amazing how much deeper our listening
can be when we're aware of our own bodies in space and feel
grounded within ourselves. This is particularly important if you
are locking eyes with someone while they're in their emotional
bit, because a lot of emotion is transmitted, and often absorbed,
through the face and eyes.

EMOTIONAL BOUNDARIES MEDITATION

If you want to practice emotional boundaries through mindfulness and breath, practice the free **Emotional Boundaries Meditation,** which you can find on my website: majomeditation.com.

In addition to mindfulness practices, a short mantra I recommend for emotional boundaries is "Feel but don't fix." I repeat this to myself when someone is coming to me with their problems, even a client. I don't fix my clients' problems, but through listening and asking powerful questions, I invite them to find their own solutions. One of the patterns I noticed with Greta was that she would feel deeply for someone, and then she would immediately rearrange her life to help them out. And it makes sense. Compassion isn't just feeling someone's pain; it's doing something to soothe it. But consider this: soothing can come from active, grounded listening, more so than from the action that follows.

I've been inspired by my clients who are mothers who consciously refrain from intervening in or fixing a situation (I mean, otherwise they'd go nuts). In one case, my client's son was upset because a classmate had taken his drawing. "I could imagine myself going down the path of marching into the class and demanding he get his drawing back." But how would that have truly helped? Her son would have learned the lesson that "Mom rescues" and that she'd later do it again. So, what did she do instead? She listened to her son's sadness and wiped his tears, which opened up the space for him to share what he wanted to do next—ask for his drawing back. Even if it feels like the hardest thing in the world to do, we can check our desire to intervene by simply listening to what another person is going through (with our emotional boundaries), which, by the way, is a great act of service in itself. The real compassion is in the mindful listening, which supports others in moving through emotion and ultimately (hopefully) feeling empowered to find their own solutions, and *not* in us "saving" others. I'm not saying never to intervene (as in a case of severe bullying, for example); I'm just saying choose your interventions sparingly.

 PRACTICE THIS MANTRA: "I FEEL BUT DON'T FIX."

Mantras work best when written out and placed somewhere. Where could you place this mantra in your life? Think bathroom mirror, car dashboard, or daily planner.

If withholding action feels impossible, experiment with it. I challenge my clients—for example: Don't volunteer. Don't help. Don't give. Don't lead this one. Let someone else step up, or let someone else pick up the pieces, and observe what unfolds. The world has been spinning without you for a long time. It's amazing to see what actually happens. *Nada malo* (nothing bad). Okay, sometimes there is a brief shit show, but it certainly isn't the apocalypse. There's a clean-up and a move-on, and everyone is ultimately just fine. It's worth your sanity and health to let go sometimes, don't you think?

Boundaries for Positive Emotions and Feedback

Let's talk about positive emotions. Emotional contagion can feel really nice, right? Like when your friend has joyful news to share. You might want some of that juju. But be careful. When we don't have emotional boundaries—even for positive emotions—it can be hard for us to understand our true feelings and thoughts about a certain event or subject because we've internalized someone else's. It can be easy for us to lose our center and fall into somebody else's high (which might lead us to be enrolled in a project to help!). Of course, some emotional contagion is inevitable, and letting it flow with awareness is the best course. The point is that we don't want to lose ourselves in other people.

Another good time to practice emotional boundaries is when someone is criticizing or praising you. When someone criticizes you so that you'll continue to do what they want, and not do what they don't want, it's time for you to separate what they're spewing onto you from what is real (that you're a worthy badass, of course). People have their baggage, and they will chuck it all over you if you're open like a public park. On the flip side, when someone is charming the heck out of you, stroking your ego, telling you how gifted you are as a way to enroll you into their company, project, or bed—you need solid boundaries. Emotional boundaries make us less vulnerable to the control and manipulation of others.

Let's talk about *constructive* praise and criticism, the kind that helps us learn and grow. I talk about this in the Myth of Perfection chapter under "Fixed Versus Growth Mind-Set," but we have to be super careful about internalizing other people's feedback as our own thoughts, beliefs, and views about the world. When we were young sponges, we had little choice (though you're reading this whole book to help you unlearn a lot of other people's shit), but as adults, we need to make our own call about things. We need to own our relationship and feelings to any given thing, place, person, event, or happening in the world. And it's completely okay to fundamentally disagree with other people's relationships to that thing. The best learning happens when we are open enough to consider other people's feedback, without blindly swallowing all of it, and mix it in with our original stance, without tossing out our original stance completely and switching over to what they said unless we truly agree with their feedback. Ideally, this will make us more complex, nuanced people—able to take on multiple perspectives instead of being black-and-white about things. In two words: filter feedback. And the best way to do that is to have emotional boundaries. You don't have to swap or sacrifice your feelings for anybody else's in order to help, please, or get along.

ONCE WE RECLAIM OUR TIME AND ENERGY, WE CAN BE OF TRUE service to others. What do I mean by *true service*? Let me tell you a quick story. A few years ago, I volunteered for a nonprofit in Ahmedabad, in the Indian state of Gujarat. The nonprofit was located beside a slum where 150,000 families lived. My hope was to support the girls and women there by teaching some stress-management tools, such as breathing exercises and meditation. The founder of the nonprofit suggested I join him and his staff on a three-day walkabout to rural villages and ashrams, sort of like a mini pilgrimage. Without hesitation, I agreed. I loved the idea of exploring a rural part of India with locals while walking under the full moon in April during the Indian Holi festival. The purpose of the walk, as he proposed it, was to witness nature, accept our circumstances, and learn more about ourselves. We would ask for food and shelter and rely on generosity and love from strangers, some of whom had very little. During this mini pilgrimage, a well-known elder in the nonprofit's community, Bala, joined us. At one point, I caught up with Bala while the others walked ahead as we passed through cotton fields on dirt roads that twisted and curved. Suddenly I noticed him bending down to pick up rocks from the road and toss them into the banks. Whenever he saw a fist-size or bigger rock, he'd kick it out of the way or bend down and chuck it. He kept doing this for about twenty minutes. I assumed it was some sort of meditation or penance. Or maybe he had obsessive-compulsive disorder. Of course, I had to know.

"Bala, why are you picking up those rocks?" I asked.

He said something that I'll never forget. It is ingrained in every fiber of my being because of how it changed my perspective on sacrifice and service.

"So that motorcyclists don't hurt themselves," he replied matter-of-factly. We hadn't even seen a motorcyclist pass through. He hadn't thought twice about it, bending his body slowly to knock rocks out of the way. He was doing something small, kind, and thoughtful for a stranger he would never meet. He was doing service, and it was no big deal. Bala expanded my idea about what service is and can be.

To call myself out here, I realized how much of my "giving" had been operating from a place of ego and obligation instead of authenticity. I went to India to teach girls and women yoga and stress management (oh, the irony) and, in a sense, was motivated by a martyr (and white savior!) complex. Too many of us good girls, especially if we're idealists, develop martyr complexes without even realizing it. People with martyr complexes are save-the-world types, and often they're evangelists who impose their perspectives on the world around them instead of letting them emerge from the people they hope to serve. Through his example, Bala showed me service can be small, anonymous, and unquantifiable. There was no way to measure his impact. He was never going to get credit for what he was doing, and that was fine.

True service emanates from the authentic self and soul. But when we're caught in the Myth of Sacrifice, we fall into reflexively helping others and giving up our time and energy out of a sense of obligation, guilt, and duty. When we feel we must give up all our time as part of our role as mother, sister, or daughter, we fall into the trap of giving up our dreams, visions, voices, and careers. While the patriarchy has expected this of us, we can choose another way. We can be more conscious and deliberate about the ways we truly want to give to the world. Like Bala, we can serve in a way that is a natural extension of who we are and an expression of our love.

Your New Toolbox

Listed here are all the tools we've explored in this chapter, along with their page numbers so you can quickly reference and practice them whenever you need to.

- Discover your time orientation: **Reactive Versus Responsive Time Orientation** (page 217).

- Reflect on nourishing versus numbing activities: **Self-Care Journaling Exercise** (page 222).

- Design a new self-care ritual: **How to Design a Self-Care Ritual (step-by-step method)** and **Behavior Design Tips** (pages 224 and 230).

- Protect yourself from others' negative emotions: **Emotional Boundaries Meditation** (page 240).

- Stop helping, fixing, or rescuing: **Feel but Don't Fix Mantra** (page 241).

For further exploration and resources, including self-care rituals and meditations for the Myth of Sacrifice, see the appendix.

9

A Journey of Integration

HEROINE, YOU'VE COME SO FAR. YOU HAVE QUESTED deep down through the swamps of your own subconscious. Hopefully, through this process you've learned that we don't slay demons in some cave on a faraway mountain but right here at home, in our own hearts and minds. The path forward isn't going to be easy but will be one of ongoing discomfort (remember: *the* sign of growth), because you're working with darker, hard-to-look-at aspects of yourself that are endlessly revealing.

Sometimes, you will wonder whether it isn't just better to put your attention on the positive, forget about it, or move on to another journey. I encourage you to keep going, even in the face of an unsettling landscape. When a caterpillar becomes a chrysalis, its entire body turns into goo in that dark cocoon before it can emerge as a new creature. Don't lose heart.

One of the harder consequences of our growth is that the people around us often change or fall away from our lives altogether. When my client Adrienne began to unravel her good girl conditioning, she shifted her role at work and left a relationship, a friendship, and her roommates to live independently for the first time in her life. She took a leap into the lonely unknown, and while in her chrysalis, she wondered whether it was worthwhile. And of course it was. In a few months, she found a more aligned partner and group of friends. If she hadn't been able to endure that messy, uncomfortable liminal space, she probably would have gone back to her old life. But because she understood the journey and is a true heroine, she withstood the discomfort for the sake of a more beautiful future.

I like to remind my clients that a heroine's journey is not a straight ascending line but a messy, zigzagging, spiraling process with backward and side steps. There is no "she lived happily ever after," because the journey never ends. Sometimes those backward steps feel small, and sometimes they feel big. After a few months into Adrienne's new life, for example, she slept with a co-worker, which made going to her job (one she ultimately didn't want) feel virtually impossible. "Am I regressing?" she wondered aloud, fighting tears, during our coaching sessions. As she was beating herself up, I reassured her that it's perfectly normal to fall, fail, and make mistakes (a.k.a. be human) and that she was standing in front of a beautiful opportunity to recommit to her journey. It's not a sign of weakness or flimsiness to fall and recommit. It's actually a sign of learning. I invited her to put her hand on her heart, close her eyes, take a deep breath, and thank herself for all her courage to date. In thanking herself, her whole system softened, and she was able to breathe easily again. Then I invited her to widen her perspective: where was she on the journey? As she reflected on the past year, she agreed she had experienced an unprecedented leap in growth. Even if she had made this embarrassing mistake, she was still growing in the direction she wanted. Adrienne eventually switched teams before quitting her job entirely.

This journey is a messy process that requires patience, since the changes we want to see happen not with a snap of our fingers but in every single moment that we catch ourselves. The moment we realize we're going along with someone else's expectations: suddenly we recognize we're snared in the Myth of Rules. The moment we observe that we're afraid to tell someone how we truly feel about a situation: we see how we're wrapped up in the Myth of Harmony. And so it goes for each myth. As we find ourselves in our good girl programming, a new space and opportunity is created to choose differently. We can pause, take a deep breath, recognize it with loving-kindness, accept it as our reality, investigate the origin of our self-sabotaging behavior, and ultimately let it go. As we move forward in the face of our fears, insecurities, and shadows, incredible new pathways unfold for us. We're no longer slaves to our unconscious, automatic good girl programming. These "alchemical" moments, seemingly insignificant instances of awareness that last only a few seconds, are the little buds for our new growth and power. It does not happen right away, but if we practice with sincerity, mindfulness, and self-compassion, we begin to realize our purpose in a way that gives us and the world meaning.

Indeed, the hardest part of this practice is accepting the uglier parts of ourselves we have long rejected, *especially* where we come from, our story, history, traumas, conditioning (even our good girl), all of which make up our humanity, no matter how complex, fragmented, or shameful they feel. Otherwise, we risk not sharing our gifts. After I challenged my client Cassidy to capture on paper her brilliant ideas about how to design more racially inclusive products, she came to our next session empty-handed. "I don't deserve to talk about this," she said matter-of-factly. "My mom's black, and my dad's white, but I grew up in Connecticut, mostly around white kids. Even today, my friends are mostly white." She paused, lost in deep thought. "I've been clinging onto labels my whole life, without ever really fitting into any of them." Even though Cassidy is infinite potential that can't be squeezed into labels, she is *also* the sum and intersections of *all* her identities (yes, a total paradox). When we add up all her identities, we make up Cassidy. As gestalt psychology teaches, the whole is greater than the sum of its parts.

In the same way, you are also the sum of *everything*. You are a mixed bag of tricks, and that's what makes you textured, colorful, beautiful, and interesting.

I like this pathway to wholeness because it allows us to see our authentic self not as the erasure of our flaws, conditioning, and shadows but as the full acceptance of them. The only way to come back to your most authentic self is to truly walk through *all* parts of yourself and love them fully. In other words, true integration. When we try so hard to fix, destroy, or get rid of any part of ourselves, it backfires in ironic fashion. It's what philosopher Alan Watts called the "law of reversed effort": Whatever you resist will typically persist.[1] Like a mouse in cream, struggling to get out only churns the cream into butter and keeps us more stuck.

When we know and accept our story, with all its ups and downs, extraordinary possibilities emerge. In fact, it's the acceptance and intersection of our many identities that offers the world new bridges and fresh perspectives we can't find anywhere else. It is because I've struggled with my good girl conditioning, and because I'm a writer, designer, Latina, immigrant, and many etceteras, that I was able to write this book. It is precisely the fact that Cassidy is a mixed-race female designer navigating mostly white spaces, who doesn't feel like she belongs, that makes her uniquely suited to speak about creating more racially inclusive experiences. While the existential angst of "Who am I?" leads us to doubt ourselves, it also leads us on to the quest to realize that it's the perceived weakness of "not belonging anywhere" that holds the gift.

This is our work as women on the journey—to befriend ourselves. Every part of yourself, including your good girl. By accepting the woman you are, you open space up for the woman you must become.

Integrated Good Girl Myths

I have good news for you: When we accept our Good Girl Myths, they begin to alchemize from their negative, shadow side into a positive, light side. As such, we can *consciously* choose to draw on them in the right contexts. We have more range and freedom. What are the unique strengths of each myth? When is it best to call on them? Let's take a look.

The Myth of Rules

"If I follow the rules, life will be easier and I will get ahead."

The strength behind rules is the ability to learn quickly as well as to adapt and be resilient in new environments. It's useful to draw on this Good Girl Myth when you are first trying to understand how a system, dynamic, discipline, or organization works, so that you can innovate on it. Rules are very useful for creativity, as the best creativity begins with and feeds off constraints.

STRENGTHS: Learning and creativity

The Myth of Perfection

"I must perform at a high level in all areas of my life without breaking a sweat."

When the Myth of Perfection is integrated, it gives us the ability to motivate and inspire ourselves. Instead of being motivated from "not good enough," we become motivated by quality, thoughtfulness, and craft. We choose perfection because of our love of beauty, not an obsession with or attachment to it. It's useful to draw on this

253

Good Girl Myth when you want to challenge yourself to create and manifest something of greater quality than you have before, not to gain others' approval but because you value excellence in whatever you're bringing to the world.

STRENGTHS: Excellence and quality

The Myth of Logic

"It's best to follow my mind and intellect over my body and intuition."

When the Myth of Logic is integrated, it makes a powerful duo and partner with your other intelligences. While intuition leads us to new possibilities, perhaps regardless of the reason (e.g., it doesn't make logical sense for me to take this new job, but I will because my gut tells me to), logic helps us figure out the "how" to get things done (once I've taken the job, what's the best way to relocate?). It's useful to draw on this Good Girl Myth when presented with information that doesn't feel intuitively right. Logic can step in and think more critically about what isn't working, ask questions, and investigate answers. In other words, logic is a great friend when we're at risk of being manipulated or taken advantage of (in this world, there's plenty of that!).

STRENGTHS: Investigation and discovery

The Myth of Harmony

"If I just go with the flow and avoid being difficult, there won't be any problems and everyone will just get along."

The strength behind harmony is the ability to put people at ease in your presence and help them feel welcome and like they belong—a true superpower! It's useful to draw on this Good Girl Myth when you want to calm and ease conflict in relationships and environments. Because women release oxytocin—a hormone that encourages soothing—in stressful situations, we have a unique ability to "tend and befriend" instead of enter into conflict with others,[2] which is the true power of harmony—but again, as long as we don't bypass the hard issues.

STRENGTHS: Nurturing relationships and peace

The Myth of Sacrifice

"I should prioritize the needs of others before my own."

The strength behind sacrifice is easy to see. There are moments when we must draw on sacrifice for something higher or that we value more. Our abilities to plan for the future in a way that is aligned with our values is an important use of this Good Girl Myth. We sacrifice one thing in the short term for something in the long term we care more about, that either feeds us or benefits those we love. Leverage this Good Girl Myth toward your goals, which often require a delay of instant gratification and a ton of discipline. The other obvious strength of this myth when it is well integrated is generosity.

STRENGTHS: Future-visioning and generosity

Collective Journey

As you walk toward wholeness, you soon realize that the journey isn't just about you and your personal growth. It's about all of us.

Your Ancestors

Remember that you are standing on the shoulders of your female ancestors. My great-grandmother on my grandfather's side was forced to do labor as a young girl in Italy, waking up at five o'clock every morning to cork wine bottles. My great-grandmother on my grandmother's side was beaten by her husband throughout her marriage and eventually was beaten to death by a thief in her home. My grandmothers had little choice but to marry and become mothers and wives. My mother, an immigrant, gave up her career and earning potential to support my father's dreams and provide more opportunities for her family and herself. These women were and are survivors. It's easy to contrast their lives with mine. When I contextualize myself in my ancestral line, I see that I can't simply squander the gifts I've been given. The women in your past, right in your ancestral line, have been through pain and hardship that is likely hard for you to imagine. When you imagine yourself standing in a long line among them, you can see that we have made progress, and we must continue to do so for our great-granddaughters.

All Women

And beyond the women in our family line, we women—regardless of where we live or come from—are on a massive, wild journey together. Though our fight is far from over, especially on behalf of low-income women and women of color, think about how far we've come in the past two hundred years. One of the *biggest* social advancements in history has been a fundamental change in the status of women since our male ancestors excluded us from participating in the most basic social activities, such as learning, voting, and owning land. To put things into perspective for a moment: in 1920—*only a hundred years ago, folks*—women secured the right to vote (though black women were blocked from exercising this right, especially in the South). It wasn't until 1969, technically after the civil rights movement, that a woman could even open a credit card without a signature from her husband (1-9-6-9!). That was only fifty years ago. We have made so much recent progress, but the job's not over, so let's not lose momentum. And let's certainly not go backward. We need the brilliance of women for emerging challenges—environmental degradation, climate change, population overgrowth, poverty, rapid globalization, data wars, pandemics, and the list goes on. As a world, we're navigating tricky waters, and we need all hands on deck.

The World Needs Your Gifts

I dream of a world where we live in true harmony in all our relationships, with other people—including those who are different from us—animals, and Mother Earth. A world in which we don't believe that we are separate from those around us but know that we are fundamentally connected. My dream is that each of us leaves this Earth stronger and more beautiful than it was when we arrived, for our children, their children, and future generations. The place to start, as Gandhi and many others have always said, is by strengthening individuals, which then ripples out to communities and cultures. And I would argue that the real place to start is by supporting women to access and unleash their power.

Many great leaders have affirmed this, with Nobel Peace Prize recipient Desmond Tutu saying, "If we're going to see real development in the world, then our best investment is women," and Michelle Obama affirming that: "The difference between a broken community and a thriving one is the presence of women who are valued." My dream is that thousands of women wake up, use their voices, and create more change so that the ripples continue toward more beauty, love, and justice. I dream that women's brilliance can be unleashed for the good of the planet.

If we women can manage the darker aspects and heal the wounds within ourselves, we can free up so much power to create change. We are beginning to glimpse the power of women when we work together and use our voices with movements such as #MeToo, Time's Up, and many more to come. Imagine what a critical mass of women who are awake, aligning their inner and outer work, could accomplish, especially if we work together. You have a key part to play in this dream.

We need more women like you sharing their gifts. Don't let the story of not being good enough or needing to fit into a certain mold stand in your way. It's time for you to do what you've been longing to do. It's time to make art. Time to be of service. Time to protest. Time to lobby. Time to preach. Time to teach. Time to sing. Time to write. Time to mother. Time to lead. Time to share. Time to discover. Time to inspire and empower others. What can you commit to starting? What can you commit to changing? How might you get more clarity about your vision? You can take more risks into the unknown. You can expand into a form of leadership that feels aligned and authentic to you. I know you can. Our Good Girl Myths will give us all the excuses in the world to keep going along with the beat of society's old drum—that we don't have enough training; that we couldn't possibly question, bend, and break away from others' rules and expectations; that we couldn't possibly design our own path and destiny; that we couldn't possibly put our controversial ideas out; that we couldn't possibly share our voices and speak our truth; that we couldn't possibly trust our bodies above all else; that we couldn't possibly risk failure and rejection; that we couldn't possibly look or be "selfish"; that we couldn't possibly become the most badass versions of ourselves, for each other and for the world—but we can. And we must. And we will.

Acknowledgments

THANK YOU TO MY HUSBAND, ENRIQUE ALLEN, FOR ALL THE TIMES you made me breakfast and brought it down to my office while I was writing. For all the dinner, phone, and text conversations about this book and for letting it be the third "person" in our marriage. You're sitting on a throne in my heart.

To my mom, dad, and brother—the nomadic Molfino tribe that gave me adventures to write about and the boundless opportunities I have today.

Bottomless thanks to my agent, Andrea Barzvi at Empire Literary, who stands by my side unconditionally. You're a badass.

Kerri Kolen, thank you for giving me full permission to be weird and voicey, at exactly the right time, and Christine Ragasa, for making the intro of a lifetime.

Thank you to my editor, Katy Hamilton, for your dedication and sharp eye, as well as your beautifully strategic and open mind. I'm so grateful you took this book baby under your wing and gave it flight. Thank you Lauren Winchester and Chantal Tom for your assistance on this journey. To the whole HarperOne team: Judith Curr, Gideon Weil, Makenna Holford, Ashley Yepsen, and the marketing and sales team, thank you for believing in me. Libby Edelson, for listening to your intuition and laying down the intellectual bones.

Special thanks as well to all the creatives on this project: Adrian Morgan for his art direction, Isabel Urbina Peña for the book cover, Janet Evans-Scanlon for the interior design, and Vanessa Koch for the special icons and other graphics.

Some more thanks to family: my *abuelitas* in Argentina for your long-distance love and light; my *tía* and *tío* in Brazil for giving me a desk and a bed to finish the manuscript; my cousin Cecilia for your late-night texting and emotional support; and my in-laws for rooting for me from the East Bay. To all my cousins, aunts, and uncles, sprinkled all over the world—I appreciate you.

I wouldn't be here without the teachers and mentors who have shaped me from close and afar. From Stanford University, I'm grateful for the influences and work of BJ Fogg, Dave Evans, Charlotte Burgess-Auburn, Karin Forssell, Jonathan Edelman, and Dan Schwartz, as well as the Learning, Design, and Technology masters program for giving me space to explore my passions for design thinking and behavior design, which inform my coaching today. In the world of women and creativity, thank you to Liz Gilbert, Cheryl Strayed, Isabel Allende, Joanna Macy, Sarah Selecky, and Clarissa Pinkola Estés, who all urge me to follow my soul's instinct when writing. Thank you to my spiritual mentors and teachers across various traditions: Tara Brach, Sweet Medicine Nation, Maya Breuer, Susana (Xochitlquetzalli), Jayesh Patel, Charles Eisenstein, Shimshai, Alan Finger, and Sri Sri Ravi Shankar, for helping me understand that love is the greatest force on the planet. Thank you to all the medicines who open my heart and mind. Thank you to all the elders who passed down their wisdom to me.

Every book needs its sisters: Nathalie Arbel, Jocelyn Blumenrose, Bernadette Cay, Kristina Ensminger, Giovanna Garcia, Kara Gates, Maria Gonzalez, Ash Huang, Ting Kelly, Elle Luna, Nisha

Moodley, Alyson Morgan, Caroline Paul, Eva Cruz Peña, Becca Pi-astrelli, Amber Rae, Rachel Rossitto, Katie Salisbury, Lianda Swain, Brittany Noel Taylor, and other book angels along the way—Farley Chase, Adam Smiley Poswolsky, and Keith Yamashita—who came in at the right phase with advice and support. Thanks to Chad Herst for reminding me that my voice and this message matter a lot, especially right now.

I'm so grateful to my private and group clients (former, too), who share their stories and lives with me, who are willing to be vulnerable to grow. I've learned as much from you as you have from me.

This book wouldn't be here if it weren't for the countless in-spiring conversations on the HEROINE podcast that helped me understand what we must overcome and reclaim for ourselves—thank you to Martha Beck, Sophia Amoruso, Randi Zuckerberg, Isabel Allende, Eileen Fisher, Luvvie Ajayi, Esther Perel, Brenda Chapman, Debbie Millman, Joy Harjo, Jessica Hische, Helena Price, Jen Sincero, Tiffany Dufu, Grace Bonney, Jessica Bennett, Ashley C. Ford, Elena Brower, Ruby Warrington, Lynsey Addario, Lisa Congdon, Roz Savage, Keiko Agena, Jaclyn Johnson, Laurie Segall, Aminatou Sow, and many more.

Thank you to Anne Hoffman, who edited the HEROINE pod-cast for many years.

And finally, to my podcast listeners and supporters—while many of us haven't met, I know some of you are breaking your Good Girl Myths as we speak.

And to you, my reader, thanks for being brave.

Appendix: Self-Care Rituals with Meditations for Each Myth

As a reminder, self-care and meditation practices can be found at majomeditation.com.

The Myth of Rules

PURPOSE OF RITUAL: Find Clarity for Your Day and Plug Into Purpose

1. Free-writing around an ingredient of meaning

2. Meditation options: Death Meditation or Breathing Exercise— Awake Breath (clears the mind)

3. Listing one to three to-dos that align with sharing your gifts

TOTAL TIME: 20–40 minutes

The Myth of Perfection

PURPOSE OF RITUAL: Soften into Self-Compassion

1. Free-writing a gratitude list

2. Meditation options: Self-Compassion Meditation or Breathing Exercise—Achiever's Cooling Breath (chilling, good for overwhelm and burnout)

TOTAL TIME: 10–20 minutes

The Myth of Logic

PURPOSE OF RITUAL: Get Out of the Mind and Drop into the Body

1. Freestyle dance

2. Meditation options: Wise Woman Within Meditation (25 minutes) or Breathing Exercise—Alternate Nostril Breath (balances the system)

3. Self-massage with oils

TOTAL TIME: 20–40 minutes

The Myth of Harmony

PURPOSE OF RITUAL: Open Your Voice and Activate Your Strength and Courage

1. Free-writing any negative feelings

2. Meditation options: Voice Activation Meditation or Breathing Exercise—Open Voice Breath (reduces anxiety and fear)

3. Core/Ab Strengthening Exercise

TOTAL TIME: 10–20 minutes

The Myth of Sacrifice

PURPOSE OF RITUAL: Connect with Pleasure and Safeguard Your Energy

1. Self-massage with oils

2. Emotional Boundaries Meditation

3. Warm bath or long shower with lavender

TOTAL TIME: 55 minutes

Notes

Chapter 1: Becoming the Good Girl

1. National Partnership for Women and Families, "Quantifying America's Gender Wage Gap by Race/Ethnicity," fact sheet, April 2019, accessed July 15, 2019, http://www.nationalpartnership.org/our-work/resources/work place/fair-pay/quantifying-americas-gender-wage-gap.pdf.

2. Marija Gimbutas, *The Prehistory of Eastern Europe, Part 1: Mesolithic, Neolithic and Copper Age Cultures in Russia and the Baltic Area*, American School of Prehistoric Research Bulletin No. 20, edited by Hugh Hencken (Cambridge, MA: Peabody Museum, 1956).

3. Gimbutas, *Prehistory*.

4. Wolfgang Haak et al., "Massive Migration from the Steppe Was a Source for Indo-European Languages in Europe," *Nature* 522, no. 7555 (2015): 207, https://doi.org/10.1038/nature14317; Iosif Lazaridis et al., "Genetic Origins of the Minoans and Mycenaeans," *Nature* 548, no. 7666 (2017): 214, https://doi.org/10.1038/nature23310.

5. Pew Research Center, "The Data on Women Leaders," Pew Social Trends fact sheet, September 13, 2018, accessed July 15, 2019, https://www.pewsocialtrends.org/fact-sheet/the-data-on-women-leaders/.

6. Martha M. Lauzen, "The Celluloid Ceiling: Behind-the-Scenes Employment of Women on the Top 100, 250, and 500 Films of 2015" (San Diego, CA: San Diego State University, Center for the Study of Women in Television and Film, 2016).

7. Center for American Women and Politics, "Women in Elective Office 2019," accessed July 15, 2019, http://www.cawp.rutgers.edu/women-elective-office-2019.

8. IDEO, "A New Venture Changes the Way We Polish Nails: Redesigning the Nail-Painting Experience for Both Hands," 2014, accessed July 15, 2019, https://www.ideo.com/case-study/a-new-venture-changes-the-way-we-polish.

9. Design for Extreme Affordability, Stanford University, "Embrace," accessed July 15, 2019, https://extreme.stanford.edu/projects/embrace/.

10. William Burnett and David J. Evans, *Designing Your Life: How to Build a Well-Lived, Joyful Life* (New York: Knopf, 2016).

Chapter 4: The Myth of Rules

1. Barbara A. Morrongiello and Theresa Dawber, "Parental Influences on Toddlers' Injury-Risk Behaviors: Are Sons and Daughters Socialized Differently?," *Journal of Applied Developmental Psychology* 20, no. 2 (1999): 227–251, https://doi.org/10.1016/S0193-3973(99)00015-5.

2. Daniel Voyer and Susan D. Voyer, "Gender Differences in Scholastic Achievement: A Meta-Analysis," *Psychological Bulletin* 140, no. 4 (2014): 1174–1204, http://dx.doi.org/10.1037/a0036620.

3. Roz Savage, "Discomfort and Risk," interview by Majo Molfino, April 19, 2016, in HEROINE: Women's Creative Leadership, Confidence, Wisdom, podcast produced by Majo Molfino, 77:08, https://podcasts.apple.com/us/podcast/discomfort-risk-roz-savage/id1100949693?i=1000367132214.

4. *The Lord of the Rings: The Return of the King*, directed by Peter Jackson (2003; Burbank, CA: New Line Cinema, 2005).

5. Alan Watts, *Tao: The Watercourse Way* (London: Souvenir Press, 2011), 31.

6. Walt Whitman, *Song of Myself* (Mineola, NY: Dover, 2001).

7. Esther Perel, "Esther Perel on Masculinity, Power, and Relationships at Work," interview by Majo Molfino, October 4, 2018, in HEROINE: Women's Creative Leadership, Confidence, Wisdom, podcast produced by Majo Molfino, 52:01, https://podcasts.apple.com/us/podcast/esther-perel-on-masculinity-power-relationships-at-work/id1100949693?i=1000421075450.

8. John Geirland, "Go with the Flow," *Wired*, September 1, 1996, https://www.wired.com/1996/09/czik/, accessed July 15, 2019.

9. Elizabeth Gilbert, *Big Magic: Creative Living Beyond Fear* (London: Bloomsbury, 2015).

10. Tom Kelley and Jonathan Littman, *The Ten Faces of Innovation: IDEO's Strategies for Beating the Devil's Advocate and Driving Creativity Throughout Your Organization* (New York: Crown Business, 2005).

11. Jake Knapp, John Zeratsky, and Braden Kowitz, *Sprint: How to Solve Big Problems and Test New Ideas in Just Five Days* (New York: Simon & Schuster, 2016), 123, Kindle.

Chapter 5: The Myth of Perfection

1. Elizabeth A. Gunderson et al., "Parent Praise to 1- to 3-Year-Olds Predicts Children's Motivational Frameworks 5 Years Later," *Child Development* 84, no. 5 (2013): 1526–1541, https://doi.org/10.1111/cdev.12064.

2. Gunderson et al., "Parent Praise."

3. William Harms, "Parents Who Praise Effort Can Bolster Children's Persistence, Self-Belief," *UChicagoNews*, February 12, 2013, https://news .uchicago.edu/story/parents-who-praise-effort-can-bolster-childrens -persistence-self-belief.

4. Carol S. Dweck, "Is Math a Gift? Beliefs That Put Females at Risk," in *Why Aren't More Women in Science? Top Researchers Debate the Evidence*, ed. Stephen J. Ceci and Wendy M. Williams (Washington, DC: American Psychological Association, 2007), 47–55, http://www.ms.uky .edu/~ma113/s.17/cdweckmathgift.pdf, accessed July 15, 2019.

5. Jennifer Henderlong, "Beneficial and Detrimental Effects of Praise on Children's Motivation: Performance Versus Person Feedback" (PhD diss., Stanford University, 2000), https://search.proquest.com /docview/304628933.

6. Edward L. Deci and Richard M. Ryan, "The Empirical Exploration of Intrinsic Motivational Processes," in *Advances in Experimental Social Psychology*, vol. 13, ed. Leonard Berkowitz (Cambridge, MA: Academic Press, 1980), 39–80.

Edward L. Deci and Richard M. Ryan, *Intrinsic Motivation and Self- Determination in Human Behavior* (New York: Plenum Press, 1985), 86.

7. Audrey Kast and Kathleen Connor, "Sex and Age Differences in Response to Informational and Controlling Feedback," *Personality and Social Psychology Bulletin* 14, no. 3 (1988): 514–523, https://doi .org/10.1177%2F0146167288143010.

8. Zachary Estes and Sydney Felker, "Confidence Mediates the Sex Difference in Mental Rotation Performance," *Archives of Sexual Behavior* 41, no. 3 (2012): 557–570, https://doi.org/10.1007/s10508-011-9875-5.

9. Tom Kelley and David Kelley, *Creative Confidence: Unleashing the Creative Potential Within Us All* (New York: Currency, 2013).

10. Cigna, "Cigna's U.S. Loneliness Index: Survey of 20,000 Americans Examining Behaviors Driving Loneliness in the United States," May 1, 2018, accessed July 15, 2019, https://www.multivu.com/players/English/8294451 -cigna-us-loneliness-survey/.

11. Harvard Medical School, National Comorbidity Survey, "NCS-R: Lifetime Prevalence Estimates," "Table 1. Lifetime Prevalence of DSM-IV/ WMH-CIDI Disorders by Sex and Cohort," 2007, accessed July 15, 2019, https://www.hcp.med.harvard.edu/ncs/ftpdir/NCS-R_Lifetime_Preva lence_Estimates.pdf.

12. Joseph L. Dieleman, Joseph L., Ranju Baral, Maxwell Birger, Anthony L. Bui, Anne Bulchis, et al. "US Spending on Personal Health Care and Public Health, 1996–2013,." *JAMA* 316, no. 24 (2016): 2627–2646, https:// doi.org/10.1001/jama.2016.16885; Craig M. Hales et al., "Prevalence of Obesity Among Adults and Youth: United States, 2015–2016," NCHS Data Brief No. 288 (Hyattsville, MD: National Center for Health Statistics, 2017), accessed July 15, 2019, https://www.cdc.gov/nchs /products/databriefs/db288.htm.

13. Roddy Scheer and Doug Moss, "Use It and Lose It: The Outsize Effect of U.S. Consumption on the Environment," *Scientific American*, accessed July 15, 2019, https://www.scientificamerican.com/article/american-consump tion-habits/.

14. Kristin Neff, *Self Compassion: Stop Beating Yourself Up and Leave Insecurity Behind* (London: Hachette UK, 2011).

Chapter 6: The Myth of Logic

1. William James, "What Is an Emotion?," *Mind* 9, no. 34 (1884): 188–205.

2. Julie Holland, "Medicating Women's Feelings," *New York Times*, February 28, 2015, accessed July 15, 2019, http://nytimes.com/2015/03/01 opinion/sunday/medicating-womens-feelings.html.

3. Brené Brown, *The Gifts of Imperfection: Let Go of Who You Think You're Supposed to Be and Embrace Who You Are* (Center City, MN: Hazelden, 2010).

4. Ronald C. Kessler et al., "The Epidemiology of Major Depressive Disorder: Results from the National Comorbidity Survey Replication (NCS-R)," *JAMA* 289, no. 23 (2003): 3095–3105, https://doi.org/10.1001/jama.289.23.3095.

5. Susan Nolen-Hoeksema, "Sex Differences in Unipolar Depression: Evidence and Theory," *Psychological Bulletin* 101, no. 2 (1987): 259–282.

6. Thomas Buckley and Alma Gottlieb, eds., *Blood Magic: The Anthropology of Menstruation* (Berkeley: Univ. of California Press, 1988), 190.

7. Buckley and Gottlieb, *Blood Magic*.

8. Michelle N. Shiota, Dacher Keltner, and Amanda Mossman, "The Nature of Awe: Elicitors, Appraisals, and Effects on Self-Concept," *Cognition and Emotion* 21, no. 5 (2007): 944–963, https://doi.org/10.1080/02699930600923668.

9. Dacher Keltner and Jonathan Haidt, "Approaching Awe, a Moral, Spiritual, and Aesthetic Emotion," *Cognition and Emotion* 17, no. 2 (2003): 297–314, https://doi.org/10.1080/02699930302297.

10. Brené Brown, *Daring Greatly: How the Courage to Be Vulnerable Transforms the Way We Live, Love, Parent, and Lead* (New York: Penguin, 2015).

11. Daniel H. Pink, *A Whole New Mind: Why Right-Brainers Will Rule the Future* (New York: Penguin, 2006), 26.

12. Anthony Perone and Artin Göncü, "Life-Span Pretend Play in Two Communities," *Mind, Culture, and Activity* 21, no. 3 (2014): 200–220, https://doi.org/10.1080/10749039.2014.922584.

Chapter 7: The Myth of Harmony

1. Lyn Mikel Brown and Carol Gilligan, *Meeting at the Crossroads: The Landmark Book About the Turning Points in Girls' and Women's Lives* (New York: Ballantine Books, 1992), 217.

2. Brown and Gilligan, *Meeting at the Crossroads*, 40.

3. Eileen Fisher, "Reclaiming the Voice," interview by Majo Molfino, August 4, 2016, in HEROINE: Women's Creative Leadership, Confidence, Wisdom, podcast produced by Majo Molfino, 53:54, http:// https://podcasts.apple.com/us/podcast/eileen-fisher-reclaiming-the-voice/id1100949693?i=1000373712256.

4. "Method: I Like, I Wish, What If," Method Cards, Stanford d.school, accessed July 15, 2019, https://dschool-old.stanford.edu/wp-content/themes/dschool/method-cards/i-like-i-wish-what-if.pdf.

5. Marshall B. Rosenberg, *Nonviolent Communication: A Language of Life*, 3rd ed. (Encinitas, CA: PuddleDancer Press), Kindle.

6. Rosenberg, *Nonviolent Communication*, locs. 1682–1686.

7. Clarissa Pinkola Estés, *Women Who Run with the Wolves: Myths and Stories of the Wild Woman Archetype* (New York: Ballantine Books, 1992), 39.

8. Estés, *Women Who Run with the Wolves*, 47.

9. Estés, *Women Who Run with the Wolves*, 49.

10. Estés, *Women Who Run with the Wolves*, 45.

11. Estés, *Women Who Run with the Wolves*, 61.

12. Luvvie Ajayi, "Speak Up and Tell Your Truth," interview by Majo Molfino, May 31, 2018, in HEROINE: Women's Creative Leadership, Confidence, Wisdom, podcast produced by Majo Molfino, 44:23, https://podcasts.apple.com/us/podcast/speak-up-tell-your-truth-luvvie-ajayi/id1100949693?i=1000412648305.

13. Audre Lorde, *Sister Outsider: Essays and Speeches* (Berkeley, CA: Crossing Press, 1984), 117.

Chapter 8: The Myth of Sacrifice

1. Darby Morhardt, "Gender Differences in Family Caregiving," research summary presentation, Cognitive Neurology and Alzheimer's Disease Center, Northwestern University Feinberg School of Medicine, 2017, accessed July 15, 2019, https://www.caregiving.org/wp-content/uploads/2017/04/9NAC-Morhardt.pdf.

2. Morhardt, "Gender Differences."

3. Twyla Tharp, *The Creative Habit: Learn It and Use It for Life* (New York: Simon & Schuster, 2008).

4. Roy F. Baumeister et al., "Ego Depletion: Is the Active Self a Limited Resource?," *Journal of Personality and Social Psychology* 74, no. 5 (1998): 1252–1265.

5. BJ Fogg, "Find a Good Spot in Your Life," *Tiny Habits*, accessed July 15, 2019, http://tinyhabits.com/good-spot.

Chapter 9: A Journey of Integration

1. Alan W. Watts, *The Wisdom of Insecurity: A Message for an Age of Anxiety* (New York: Vintage, 1951).

2. Shelley E. Taylor et al., "Biobehavioral Responses to Stress in Females: Tend-and-Befriend, Not Fight-or-Flight," *Psychological Review* 107, no. 3 (2000).